Ansley J. Coale

Ansley J. Coale

Ansley J. Coale

An Autobiography

AMERICAN PHILOSOPHICAL SOCIETY

2000

MEMOIRS

of the

AMERICAN PHILOSOPHICAL SOCIETY

Held at Philadelphia
For Promoting Useful Knowledge

VOLUME 236

LIBRARY OF CONGRESS CATALOGING-IN-PUBLICATION DATA

Coale, Ansley J.
  Ansley J Coale: an autobiography.
    p. cm.—(Memoirs of the American Philosophical Society held at Philadelphia
  for promoting useful knowledge, ISSN 0065-9738; v. 236)
  Includes bibliographical references and index.
  ISBN 0-87169-236-8 (hc)
    1. Coale, Ansley J. 2. Demographers—United States—Biography. 3.
  Economists—United States—Biography. I. Title. II. Memoirs of the American
  Philosophicalk Society; v. 236.

Q11.P612 Vol. 236
[HB865.C63A3]
304.6'092—dc21
[B]

                                                                    99-087224

ISBN: 0-87169-236-8   US ISSN: 0065-9738

CONTENTS

$\mathcal{A}$BBREVIATIONS

To help readers not familiar with demographic institutions, what follows is a list of abbreviations used in this manuscript.

AID   U.S. Agency for International Development

CAPMAS   Egyption Central Agency for Public Mobilization and Statistics

CELADE   U.N. Center for Latin American Demography

GNP   Gross National Product

IUSSP   International Union for the Scientific Study of Population

LDC   Less-developed country

MDC   More-developed country

MIT   Massachusetts Institute of Technology

NAS   National Academy of Sciences

OPR   Office of Population Research, Princeton University

PAA   Population Association of America

RadLab   Radiation Laboratory, MIT

SSRC   Social Science Research Council

UNFPA   United Nations Fund for Population Activity

WFS   World Fertility Survey

$\mathcal{I}$NTRODUCTION

THIS AUTOBIOGRAPHY is written by an 82-year-old retired professor, whose memory is failing, and who lacks systematic documentation of his life. Writing an autobiography was suggested by my 49-year-old younger son when I complained about the frustration of spending hours each day looking for manuscripts or books that I had just had in hand, and about finding it difficult to deal with mathematical reasoning that not long ago seemed quite simple. He suggested that I complete the project I was working on and then write the story of my life. His proposal did sound like a pleasant change in activity, and I hope that the result will not bore all potential readers. The basic theme is the intellectual aspects of my life, including features of my formal education from primary school through graduate school and also my years studying and teaching radar while in the Navy. The major part of the discussion concerns demography: my own involvement in population studies from graduate school to the present, the evolution of the field during the past 55 years and my role in developing and teaching this science.

I

$\mathcal{E}$ARLY YEARS OF MY LIFE

I WAS BORN in Women's Hospital in Baltimore in November of 1917. In the fall of 1923 I entered the first grade of the Calvert School, a well-known private elementary school that had a unique curriculum and method of teaching. It provided parents (such as missionaries living abroad) with teaching material that could be used for a correspondence course in parental instruction at home. Part of the school's approach was to learn by doing: on the first day of the first grade we printed "I SEE" repeatedly in large letters. As the year progressed, *we* progressed to printing in capitals, then in small letters, and then to writing script, while also advancing in reading and arithmetic. We even had lessons in oral French, of which I recall only Mademoiselle saying harshly "Do not interrompt me!"

The school preserved our daily written work and at the end of the year bound it as a permanent record. I find it remarkable that by the second semester of the first grade we were adding and subtracting two digit numbers and starting to use fractions. We also had progressed to writing short essays, of which I offer one example. Evidently the class was asked in the second half of the first grade to write a series of essays on topics beginning with "zoo" and proceeding through a list of animals. Here is what I wrote about *The Fox*: "Once a hunter tried to catch a fox but the fox hid behind a tree and it was night and the hunter could not see the tree and shot and came to get a dead fox had a bag and had a chicken in the bag and did not know it because it had flown in the bag and the fox ate the chicken and all was well with the fox." From a six year old we get childish humor and punctuation and somewhat childish spelling, but I think the early start in writing prose was nevertheless valuable.

On November 10, 1924 we moved to Cleveland—after my first grade in the Calvert School, but brother Jim went through third grade. (His third grade workbook includes several-page essays on features of classical Rome.)

While we were living in Baltimore, my father took a position as summer pastor in a church in Emmitsburg, a small town in western Maryland. A memorable feature of this summer was a one day visit to the battlefield at Gettysburg, only a few miles away. I still remember features of this tour (including Little Round Top, Big Round Top, and Devil's

Den), but I remember especially our guide, who was a veteran of the battle! (It had taken place only about 60 years before).

After we moved to Cleveland, my father served as head of the Federation of Presbyterian Churches of the city. We moved into half of a double house (11011 Clifton Boulevard) in the western part of Cleveland, two or three blocks from Lake Erie. My sister enrolled in the local high school, and Jim and I in the fourth and second grades of the Fruitland Elementary School. The Fruitland School was not the equal of Calvert, but it was excellent. I remember a large 16-year old boy in the sixth grade who used to bully the normal–sized elementary school students. He had been held back several times for failures in required subjects. According to the superficial psychology that now dominates many public school systems, keeping him back with younger children was a mistake, because of the damage to his ego. But when he finished the sixth grade, his command of reading, writing, and arithmetic (plus geography and history) was at the sixth grade level. How much worse for his self respect (and, I think, for his character) would it have been to arrive in junior high school unable to read the text books or to do simple arithmetic, even if he were among fellow students of his own size and age?

Annapolis High School and Mercersburg

In 1928 we moved to Annapolis, Maryland, where my father was to be pastor of the Presbyterian Church. Starting in 1930, I attended the public high school in Annapolis for four years. I intended to enroll in Princeton, where Jim entered in 1933. The entrance requirements included a satisfactory record in a qualified secondary school, and satisfactory results on College Entrance Board examinations in required fields, which included Latin, a modern language, algebra, plane and solid geometry, trigonometry, and two sciences. A candidate was allowed to take the College Boards in individual subjects as he completed each one, rather than all together at the end of secondary school. I passed my boards in math and sciences, but had trouble with Latin. In the Annapolis High School, the introductory Latin course in Freshman year, and the second year course including Caesar, were offered every year; but the advanced courses covering Cicero and Vergil were given in alternate years. In my third year Vergil was offered, and I received good grades. When I took the College Board in Vergil, however, I scored only 28 percent. Since this was not acceptable for admission, and I was to be only 16 on graduation from high school, my parents explored the possibility of a year in a good preparatory school. Fortunately, the Mercersburg Academy had an unusual policy of admitting some students for just one year, and also had a generous scholarship program for boys from low–income families; and I was accepted. My father insisted that I complete my study of Latin by taking the course in Cicero offered at Mercersburg. I did, and at the end of the year received a 96 percent in the College Board on Cicero.

This happy outcome of my Mercersburg course in Latin is only a minor part of the intellectual stimulus I received from the school. For example, I took two semesters of English from Archibald Rutledge, who had been named poet laureate of North Carolina. He gave us a deep appreciation of the several plays of Shakespeare that we studied, and of other great poetry and prose. One day every week, we wrote an original essay, or made comments on some literary gem he presented to us. We wrote in a notebook, which he collected and later returned, with his editing and comments. Reexamining the notebook, I still marvel at Rutledge's skillful comments and fine insights.

Another extraordinary teacher was Mr. Chapman, who taught American history. In his course we also had to write a weekly theme, but always on an assigned topic. After the essay had been written, he asked one student to read his version aloud. He made editorial comments, such as asking "What was the date?" If the account included a treaty or a law, he insisted that the principal provisions be listed, with numbers (1,2,3,4). All of the students had to take note of his comments, and have a corrected copy of the essay in their notebooks. On any later examination, the points he had suggested had to be listed in full. Picture one of Chapman's students taking a college board exam, and being asked a question about the Monroe Doctrine. His answer would include the relevant dates, and the principal provisions of the Doctrine (1,2,3,4). I found Chapman's method for organizing material useful through the rest of my education, and even to this day.

As I recall, about one third of the class that graduated from Mercersburg in 1935 entered Harvard, Yale, or Princeton. I made many warm friends in this one year of prep school, so that in addition to its contributions to my intellectual development, and the memorable good times I had, I had eighteen companions from Mercersburg when I arrived for my freshman year in College.

Summer Employment while a Student

In my teens, I felt the need for extra funds, and recall several summer jobs I held. The father of one of the neighborhood boys about our age was president of the Annapolis Dairy Products Company, a successful local enterprise. Three members of the "Taney Avenue gang" took advantage of personal acquaintance to get summer jobs with this company delivering milk and ice to Sherwood Forest, a resort on the Severn, six or seven miles from Annapolis. We would pick up a 1.5-ton truck at the dairy at about 2 a.m., load it with 300-pound slabs of ice, and many cases of milk. We drove to a storehouse belonging to the dairy, located at Sherwood Forest. We stored the ice in the insulated warehouse, to be picked up for later delivery, and started delivering milk. One of us would drive the truck, and the other two would go from summer cottage to summer cottage dropping off the milk on order. Then we returned to the warehouse, split the 300-pound ice slabs into three 100-pound chunks, loaded them on the truck, and started delivering ice. The typical order was 25 or 50 pounds; we split the 100-pound chunks into these smaller pieces and took them into the iceboxes in the cottages. When we were finished, we returned the truck to the dairy, and walked home, arriving at about 5 p.m., with feet wet from dripping ice. I remember going to the dairy at 2 a.m, sometimes with shoes still wet from the day before, and on my way meeting friends who were on a late night out. For seven days of this labor, we were paid $12. I quit after two weeks; soon thereafter separate crews were employed to deliver ice and to deliver milk.

Another summer job I had in Annapolis was provided, like the job of milkman and iceman, by the father of one of the Taney Avenue gang. Phil Weems's father, Commander Weems, had been a specialist in navigation before his retirement from the Navy. He had trained famous aviators, including Amelia Earhart, Post and Gatty, and Charles Lindbergh, in celestial navigation, and was devising a procedure to permit navigation using the stars without any mathematical calculations. The standard calculations took at least several minutes, and involved use of tables for spherical trigonometry. These features made celestial navigation of limited usefulness for aviators, especially when flying alone at high speed. During the 1930s, then, Commander Weems developed what he called star altitude curves, which presented the relevant information graphically. He imagined a stationary transparent sphere that fitted over the surface of the earth, under which the earth rotated. He then calculated the locus of points on this sphere, points that had a series of given angles of elevation for several prominent fixed stars. Given the elevations of two fixed stars, one can find at the intersection of two star altitude curves the longitude and latitude of this point, on the hypothetical fixed sphere. The latitude on the real earth is the same, and the real longitude can be determined by the correct reading of Greenwich Mean Time, provided by a precise chronometer. Pete Fox and I spent part of one summer using old–

fashioned mathematics and tables to calculate the star altitude curves. These were then plotted and assembled in a book that would make celestial navigation much simpler and faster. The developments in radio and electronics during and after WWII have totally displaced these plots and most other dependence on celestial navigation.

One summer (I cannot recall if it was before or after I entered college) I learned that a teen-age girl who was finishing a private secondary school had failed to graduate because she had failed plane geometry. I negotiated the job of tutoring her so that she could take a make-up exam. After reviewing Euclid's principal theorems and giving her a number of originals to prove, I learned that I was to administer an examination that I made up for her. I constructed an exam asking her to state one of the theorems, and to prove three or four propositions that I made up. When these questions had been typed, I decided to tell the girl that I was giving her a practice examination, and that she was to treat it as the real thing, so as to get used to the ordeal. I graded the paper and sent it to the school, explaining that I accepted her inexactly–quoted version of the theorem and of the "reasons" for the points in the proof, because I felt the principles of demonstration were important, but that memorizing statements was not. In return I received a letter saying that my pupil had been judged to have made up her deficiency. The letter was addressed to "Professor Coale."

II

*C*OLLEGE YEARS

I ARRIVED on the Princeton Campus by train; subsequent trips from home to college were by hitch-hiking. I moved into a single room in an old dormitory built in the 1870s, and named Reunion Hall, after the reconciliation of the Northern and Southern Presbyterian Churches at the end of the Civil War. In addition to the companionship of my Mercersburg friends, I profited from the presence (in the next entry of Reunion) of my brother and his roommate, Henry Schneider, who as Juniors could readily guide a Freshman over some of his first–year bumps.

Undergraduate Years at Princeton

While still at Mercersburg and applying for college admission, I had asked for a scholarship, essential because of our family's low income and its need to support my older brother already in college. I received a letter from the Princeton scholarship office, saying that my name and application had been given to Richard Cleveland, an attorney in Baltimore charged with administering the Armstrong Scholarships. These scholarships provided for the support of one student from Maryland and one from Michigan at any given time. Mr. Cleveland invited me to come see him, and told me I had been awarded the Armstrong Scholarship for a Maryland resident (provided of course that I was admitted to the university).

The Armstrong stipend was $625 per year; tuition plus fees came to $550; thus the scholarship covered tuition plus a substantial part of room rent, less than $100 in the least expensive dormitories. To pay for meals I worked as a waiter in the college dining halls, where the underclassmen were obliged to take their meals (at a cost of $8 per week). The waiters were paid 28 cents per table, with a bonus for working more than 10 meals, including a specified number of breakfasts. Depending on the number of waiters who showed up at the same meals, about 10–14 meals of waiting would usually cover the board.

In my sophomore year I found another way to earn income. There were a number of student agencies under the Student Employment Office that were given something like a monopoly to provide certain services on the campus. One such agency was the student tutoring agency. An official student tutor in a given subject was designated by the student head of the agency, presumably after competition to select a well qualified candidate. One of Jim's classmates had been chosen as tutor in the introductory course in psychology, and had done well in the tutoring in his junior year. In his senior year, faced with the need to write a thesis, he found the work to prepare his tutoring formidable. I had taken Psychology 201 and 202 as a freshman, with top grades. He proposed that we work together in preparing tutoring notes, and that I do the actual teaching. He got the agency to approve this scheme, and I earned more from the tutoring than from waiting on tables. The next year I cited my experience when I applied successfully for the position of Student Agency tutor in introductory psych. In my senior year (my second as the designated tutor in the psychology course), a student who was son of a prominent alumnus failed in almost all of the first "hour exams" in his five sophomore courses. His father went to see one of the deans about this crisis, and the dean suggested engaging student tutors who might help the poor student learn how to study more effectively. The manager of the agency called in the relevant course tutors and told us to go all out to bring up the young man's performance in the second hour tests in all of his subjects. I suggested to him that he attend the wholesale review session in psychology that I offered for students who did not want individual treatment, and then that he arrange for additional individual instruction.

The professor who taught the course announced that material from the lectures and the text books would be covered by short answer questions, but that there would be an essay question on each of the two "outside reading" books, and each student must answer the question on the book he had chosen to read.

I prepared an outline of the material likely to be covered in the short answer questions, and then composed a brief statement of the principal theme in each of the "outside readings." I told the students that the essay question would, in fairness, ask about something closely related to the theme. I suggested that if they mastered the essence of my brief statement, they could write a brief paragraph linking the question to the theme, and then swing into what they could remember of my statement.

In my individual tutoring of the desperate young son of the Princeton alumnus, I asked him to write an answer to what I thought was a typical essay question on the outside book he had read. Even with my brief statement of the theme of the book before him, he could not compose a good answer. I wrote out a good answer, and suggested he print it firmly in his mind. On the hour test, the essay question was almost verbatim the same as my "typical question." My tutee rose from failure on the first hour test to B+ on the second. The professor asked me to come to his office, and inquired if I had tutored the student. When I replied yes, he said that he knew it. After all, psychologists know something about the constancy of the IQ. He added that the final exam would be so designed that tutoring would be no help. In fact he announced this plan at the last lecture; but it was poor psychology; the large turnout in my tutoring review session for the final exam was unprecedented. Negative advertising can promote sales.

Undergraduate Academic Experience at Princeton

On the basis of my own studies as a Princeton undergraduate, I give somewhat unusual advice to young people about what they should study in college. I begin by recommending a liberal arts institution rather than a technical school and say that they should be guided by what interests them and what will broaden their intellects rather than what will prepare them for a career. I remember a relevant interchange with a motorist who picked me up when I was hitchhiking in the spring of my senior year. He asked what I was doing with my life. I explained that I was a senior at Princeton. Then he asked what was my major, and I said economics. Then he wanted to know what I was going to do after graduation, and I said that I did not know. "Then why are you studying economics?" I replied that I might end up as a shoeclerk, but at least I would be able to read the New York Times.

In my freshman year, anticipating a major in math or physics, I signed up in advanced sections in calculus and physics. My teacher in calculus was Luther Eisenhardt, chairman of the math department and dean of the graduate school. The lecturer in the physics course (and teacher in the class section to which I was assigned) was Henry Smyth, later author of "The Smyth Report" on the development of atomic energy. I took an obligatory course in English literature, taught by Osgood, the departmental chairman. The other two courses I selected were a survey of French literature beginning in the late Renaissance and continuing into the twentieth century (in the second semester we were assigned a novel each week), and the introductory course in Psychology, discussed at an earlier point.

In my sophomore year I continued with advanced calculus, and with physics. I tried to broaden my background by taking introductory biology, introductory German, and music appreciation. The courses in biology and music were taught by senior professors who were voted each year as among the most popular lecturers. One of the outstanding features of undergraduate education at Princeton is that the best known senior professors devote a major part of their time and energy to teaching undergraduates, teaching that includes individual supervision of the students' independent work in their junior and senior years.

In my second year, a semi-accidental event led to my switching into the introductory course in economics, and to my deciding that that subject would be my major. The accident happened in the music course taught by Professor Welsh. Welsh made the course memorable by teaching the structure of musical compositions. He would play a piece on the piano (or on a recording) and have the students write down the sequence of themes (such as aaba), and he would explain the subtlety of the variations. He told us that the highest appreciation of music was intellectual, not sensual. On the first hour test, he played several compositions, and asked us to identify the music and its composer, and to diagram its structure. I received a very poor grade, and thought I must have a tin ear, and should not jeopardize my scholarship by continuing the music course to the end of the semester. My roommate was taking the introductory course in economics; when I read the textbook assignments for the first few weeks, and looked at the questions on the first hour test, economics looked like a field I could readily master. So I managed to switch from my music course to the first course in economics. When the music hour test was returned, it turned out that I had done fine on identification and diagraming of compositions; I had fallen down on the outside–reading question because I had skimped the reading.

At the end of sophomore year I chose economics rather than math or physics as my major because I had mastered the introductory courses readily, found the substance interesting, and perhaps was moved by the social relevance of economics in the ongoing economic depression.

In my junior and senior years I supplemented the required economics upperclass courses, and the required independent work (junior papers and senior thesis), with upperclass math and physics courses as electives. I also continued a search for broader intellectual assets by taking modern European history and the roots of the English language.

Entrance into Graduate School and Meeting Sarah Campbell

In the spring of my senior year I realized belatedly that I had made no plans for what I would do after graduation. I soon decided that I should continue my studies by entering graduate school. To reverse (partially) my earlier decision to move from math or physics to economics I thought of pursuing graduate study in mathematical economics, which in 1939 was not yet a conventional field. I went to see Professor Eisenhardt, Dean of the Graduate College, to get his advice about where I might apply to study mathematical economics. Eisenhardt was also chairman of the mathematics department, and had been my teacher in freshman math. He said that I should look for first-rate universities that had strong departments in both economics and mathematics, mentioning Harvard and Chicago as possibilities. In the end he said I should probably apply to the Princeton graduate school, because the high quality economics faculty included Professor Oscar Morgenstern who was working with the brilliant mathematician Von Neumann to develop the highly mathematical theory of games. The mathematics department at Princeton was then unsurpassed.

A few days later I received a note from Eisenhardt saying that I should go see Frank Notestein, who was director of the Office of Population Research, which had been established three years earlier at Princeton. The Office administered a graduate fellowship to be awarded to a PhD candidate in economics who was willing to include demography as one of the five fields in which he would elect to be examined in the required PhD general examinations. The fellowship covered full expenses for a graduate student, and when it was offered to me I happily accepted. I had no good idea of what population study was. Thus I started in economics because I was afraid of losing my scholarship from ineptitude in music, and entered demography because of the chance to obtain a generous fellowship.

Sue Coale (nee Sarah Hamilton Campbell)

One of my best friends among my undergraduate classmates was Walter Daub. In the spring of our senior year he told me that his first cousin, a junior at Goucher College in Baltimore, was an exceptional person both in looks and personal qualities, and that I should meet her. On May 15, 1939 I was hitchhiking home in Annapolis for the weekend. Whoever had given me a ride to Baltimore dropped me on North Avenue. My sister had gone to Goucher, and I remembered that the dormitory where Walter said his cousin lived was not far away. I walked to the building and asked the receptionist if I could see Sarah Campbell. Down the stairs came an extremely attractive young woman, wearing a skirt and sweater, white socks, and saddle shoes. I told her who I was, and explained that the next day I planned to go in the family car from Annapolis to College Park, where Princeton was scheduled to play the University of Maryland in lacrosse. My roommate, Johnny Matthews, was the goaltender on the lacrosse team. I asked Sue (she had been named for one grandmother, but insisted on a shortened version of the other grandmother's name) if I could pick her up at the dorm the next day, go to the lacrosse game, and then have a picnic supper for the three of us. Sue became (and remains) the most valued and most loved person in my life. We became engaged after a few months and married in October, 1941.

After we became engaged and while I was a graduate student, we had a serious disagreement. Sue's father had sold his steel barrel plant for a large sum, and was setting up trust funds for each of his daughters. Frank Graham, a much admired economics professor who taught me both undergraduate and graduate courses, had written about ethical issues in economics. He felt that there was an ethical justification for differences in income, because different persons made contributions that society valued differently. Persons who inherited wealth, however, had done nothing for society, so Graham felt there should be a one hundred percent inheritance tax. Reflecting this view, I said to Sue that she should deed her trust fund to charity. She disagreed, and we were both upset. I described the situation to Frank Notestein, my closest friend among my professors, and he said that I could doubtless out argue Sue on this issue, but asked whether I felt I had a right to impose my views on her. I replied "No," and remain grateful to Notestein for his correct advice. Sue has used her inheritance for discreet and generous purposes. For most of the years since our marriage, she has uncomplainingly lived at the modest level supportable by the meager pay of a junior naval officer and an academic. When it became necessary for me to visit many countries for research, consulting, and lecturing, and when our two boys were adult (or nearly so) she did draw on her inherited resources to travel with me. It has been a great pleasure for me to have her company, and to have her guidance to the best sights in foreign cities after I have finished my professional responsibilities there.

My Initiation as Milbank Fellow at the Office of Population Research

I earlier explained that I chose to enter the graduate college at Princeton because of the availability of a full fellowship provided by the Office of Population Research for a PhD candidate in economics, if I were willing to offer population studies as one of the five fields for the PhD general examinations. When the director of the Office, Frank Notestein, offered me the Milbank Fellowship, explaining that it provided support for summers as well as the academic year, he also told me that the Fellow must provide clerical help to the office in the summer and part time during the months when classes met. My formal association with demography thus began the day after the graduation exercises at which I received a BA in economics.

The clerical work for the Milbank Fellow was principally helping in the production of *Population Index*, a bibliographical quarterly published by the OPR. In those early days, the founding editor of the Index, Irene Taeuber, a senior professional demographer employed by the OPR, lived in Washington and spent part of her time at the Library of Congress preparing abstracts of books and articles of interest to demographers. These abstracts arrived on slips of paper, and were typed (with dark ribbons for photo-offset reproduction) by the secretary. The typed text was proofread against Taeuber's slips by a research assistant and the Milbank fellow. I recall two errors, one that Dudley Kirk and I caught, and another that we made. The error we caught was an item in a foreign language on the incidence of tuberculosis in *mus musculus albinus*, which Irene had translated as the incidence in Mus Musculus, Albania. Fortunately one of us remembered enough Latin to recognize "white mouse," and we deleted this item. The mistake that Dudley and I made was in composing a summary of a new French law on population. The law included the regulation of "maisons d'accouchement"; Dudley and I, thinking "how French!" translated the houses being regulated as houses of prostitution (caught by the secretary).

In September of 1939, after spending the summer in proofreading and other clerical work at the Office of Population Research and hitchhiking with Johnny Matthews to Los Angeles in a visit to Sue and her friend (who were taking summer courses at USC), I began taking graduate courses in economics as a candidate for the PhD. These courses came to include micro and macro economic theory, the history of economic thought, money and banking, international trade, labor economics, mathematical statistics, and, of course, the study of population. I was privileged to have instruction from original and productive scholars who were also gifted teachers, and to learn in small seminars in the company of some brilliant students, several of whom have become creative intellectual leaders. One of my professors that fall introduced me to the area in which I have done most of my own original research: Frank Notestein implanted an unending curiosity about demographic interrelations, and about the causes and consequences of population trends.

IV

$\mathcal{F}$RANK W. NOTESTEIN

FRANK NOTESTEIN was so important in my life, and was such a close friend that I feel obliged to devote a chapter of this autobiography to the story of his life. This section is drawn from a biographical sketch that I composed for the American Philosophical Society *Proceedings* after Frank's death in 1983.

Notestein was born in Alma, Michigan, in 1902, the son of Frank Newton Notestein, who was professor of mathematics and dean of the faculty at Alma College. His great grandfather, Jonas Notestein, had founded a local academy, and his grandfather taught there. Despite this intellectual background, his boyhood was a normal small-town midwestern one. He played football and served as captain of the military company at the Alma High School, and worked in a pickle factory and as a general assistant in the local furniture store during his summer vacations. Even when he had achieved international prominence, he never fully lost his small-town air, which was revealed in such phrases as "That's not my line of country," or "That sticks in my craw."

He spent his college freshman year at Alma and then transferred to Wooster College in Ohio, where he majored in economics, and became engaged to Daphne Limbach who was queen of May in her senior year. After graduating from Wooster, Notestein entered Cornell from which in 1925 he received his PhD in social statistics. At Cornell he was introduced to demography by Walter Willcox, who aroused Notestein's interest in population, and also engendered an appreciation of the value of simplicity and the importance of thorough knowledge of one's basic data. These attitudes were evident in all of Notestein's scientific work, and were transmitted to most of his own students. While still a graduate student, Notestein was asked by Willcox (who served as advisor to the Milbank Memorial Fund) to examine the success of the Milbank Fund's health demonstration project in Cataraugus County, a project designed to reduce the death rate from tuberculosis. Already exhibiting the skepticism that characterized his thinking throughout his career, Notestein found little difference in the reduction of mortality rates in Cataraugus county and in control counties with no special health program.

After completing his PhD, Notestein married Daphne Limbach, who was his wife, close companion, and most dependable advisor until his death 56 years later. The newlyweds spent a year in Europe, where Notestein studied occupational mortality on a Social Science Research Council fellowship. In 1928, Edgar Sydenstricker offered Notestein his first professional position as a research associate at the Milbank Memorial Fund. Sydenstricker had become head of the research program at Milbank, after having set up the statistical programs of the U.S. Public Health Service, and the League of Nations. He had had the foresight, despite Notestein's unwelcome findings about the Fund's health demonstration project, to hire this graduate student in the summer of 1926 to tabulate special vital statistics from New York State, and to allow him to use the statistics for his dissertation.

As a professional employee of the Milbank Fund, Notestein began his fundamental contributions to modern demography. His first work (in collaboration with Sydenstricker) was a study of class differences in fertility in the United States, based on returns of the 1910 census. Notestein went to the Census Bureau in Washington, where he was appointed a special agent, because the confidentiality rules of the Bureau forbade access to individual census returns by nonemployees; employees were sworn under penalty not to reveal individual information. He drew a special sample of about seventy thousand native-white married women who had responded to a question asked in 1910 about the number of children each woman had borne. In the 1930s his continued research on differential fertility produced several basic articles on the subject, including a notable analysis of the fertility of families on relief, a topic of importance in the 1930s because of the common belief that the improvident poor accepted public subsidy and then had more children than they otherwise would. Notestein showed that the high fertility of those on relief could be completely explained by various selection factors determining who was on relief, and that there was no basis for supposing that in the 1930s relief increased the fertility of its recipients.

The other major research area that Notestein entered while at Milbank was investigation of the part that contraception played in the reduction in fertility generally known by the 1930s to have occurred in most of Europe, as well as in the United States and other overseas areas inhabited by Europeans. In the 1920s and 1930s many biologists and biometricians (such as Raymond Pearl and Corrado Gini) believed that population trends were caused mostly by biological influences, especially population density. Social scientists looked for social explanations. Some social scientists attributed both the general decline in fertility and class differences in fertility to the diffusion of contraceptive technology, as effective techniques were adopted first by more educated upperclasses, but then spread to less educated, lower socioeconomic categories. Others emphasized the changed attitude toward procreation that occurs in modernized societies less dominated by tradition, societies in which social advancement is possible, in which women have opportunities outside the house, and in which education is nearly universal.

Notestein used direct evidence to prove the importance of attitude rather than biology or new contraceptive technology in the decline of fertility in populations of European origin. In collaboration with Dr. Regine Stix, he initiated a follow-up study of patients from the Margaret Sanger Clinic in New York. They found that in the absence of contraception, American women would have as high a birth rate as any on record. Moreover, most of the older married couples had relied on *coitus interruptus* and had thereby achieved much lower fertility than would have occurred without contraception. From these and other first-hand observations, Notestein concluded that it had been a change in attitude, and not merely the invention of modern contraceptives, that had caused the birth rate to fall. He noted that greater desire to reduce fertility could as well be called the cause of modern methods, as these methods could be called the cause of lower fertility. Obviously both were important.

These inferences from direct evidence supported a clearer and more soundly based statement of the "demographic transition" than earlier formulations. The demographic transition is the name given to changes in birth and death rates that typically accompany the transformation of a society from a traditional agriculturally-based structure to a modern technologically–based industrial structure. Notestein's first statement describing (and accounting for) the transitional reduction in mortality and fertility appeared in *Controlled Fertility* (1940) reporting his work with Dr. Stix. The most fully developed version was in a paper "Economic Problems of Population Change" presented in 1953 at the eighth international conference of agricultural economists.

The demographic transition had been perceived and its description elaborated by several other authorities (some well in advance of Notestein's work), but the clear demonstration that the decline in fertility was not of biological origin, and the delineation of the role of attitudes, constitute his crucial contributions. Notestein also perceived at an early date that the relation between social change and population trends (the demographic transition) that had been found in the history of the wealthier, more industrialized countries implied a potential for very rapid growth in population in the less developed countries. Even before World War II he taught his graduate students that social and economic progress in India and Indonesia (for example) would bring a reduction in death rates long before there would be any decline in the birth rate. The enlarged gap between birth and death rates constitutes more rapid growth in population. Because some of the areas in which he foresaw rapid growth were very poor and already very densely settled, he feared these demographic tendencies would themselves be an impediment to progress. These prophetic ideas were published in the mid-1940s, well before most observers had any notion that an explosive growth of numbers in the less developed countries was about to begin.

In 1936 Notestein left the Milbank Fund to become the founding director of the Office of Population Research at Princeton, where he became in due time a professor of demography. At Princeton, in addition to developing his ideas on the demographic transition and its implications for less developed countries, he carried out, or fostered, much research on international population trends. Among the fruits of this body of research were four books on the population of Europe written for the League of Nations, and two major books on Asia, one on India (by Kingsley Davis) and one on Japan (by Irene Taeuber), instigated by the Office of the Geographer in the State Department.

Notestein combined his interest in international population studies with his insight into the prospective rapid growth implied by the demographic transition when he served as a member of a group (the others were Irene Taeuber, Marshall Balfour, and Roger Evans) that in 1948 conducted a survey of health and population problems in the Far East. The group, financed by the Rockefeller Foundation, traveled through Indonesia, the Philippines, Taiwan, Korea, Japan, and China. In its discussion of China, their report emphasized the potential for rapid growth. At the time of their visit China was still under the Nationalist government, had not recovered from the ruinous effects of World War II, and was already engaged in a civil war. The report, written on their return to the United States and after the victory of the Communists in the civil war, foresaw the possibility of rapid growth, because the health program that might be implemented if the new government proved effective, could reduce the death rate dramatically, but Chinese traditions of high fertility would change only slowly. The rapid growth of the population of the People's Republic (interrupted by high mortality and reduced fertility following the disastrous Great Leap Forward and arrested only by the increasingly stringent anti-fertility campaign since 1970) shows the extraordinary prescience of the report.

Two features of Notestein's career other than his scientific contributions merit explicit mention. He was a superb builder of institutions and an exceptional teacher. His affiliation with the Milbank Memorial Fund ended as he undertook his first major creation of a successful pathbreaking institution. Frederick Osborn, who had retired when still in his thirties from a successful business career to undertake social science research, played a role in Notestein's first exercise in institution building, a role that Osborn was to play many times in his long life—the role of successful promoter in the social sciences. He persuaded the Milbank Fund to provide the finances and Princeton University to provide the intellectual home for a new research organization in demography—the Office of Population Research. In 1936, Notestein came to Princeton as the organizing director of the Office, which was the first university-based unit for research and graduate training in demography. When founded, the Office consisted of its director, a secretary, a research associate, and a graduate student who held the Milbank Memorial Fund fellowship. Irene Taeuber worked in Washington as editor of *Population Index*, a bibliographical quarterly that the Office took over soon after Notestein came to Princeton and still publishes today. Although it never had a very large staff (a maximum of ten or twelve professional demographers, at most times fewer), the Office established a solid reputation for innovative work on diverse aspects of demography: the causes and consequences of population trends, particular studies of the population of many countries and regions, contributions to formal and mathematical demography, methods of measurement and projection, and analytical and empirical research on fertility, mortality, nuptiality, and age structure. The staff that Notestein recruited over the years at Princeton—among them Irene Taeuber, Frank Lorimer, Dudley Kirk, Kingsley Davis, John Hajnal, Robert Potter, and Charles Westoff—and the students he trained—among them John Durand, Norman Ryder, Harvey Leibenstein, Alvaro Lopez, and Paul Demeny—would find a place in any history of the development of the modern study of population. Both colleagues and students were in some degree infected by his skepticism, respect for evidence, and insistence on rigor and technical competence.

In 1946 Notestein, on half-time leave of absence from Princeton for two years, helped establish the Population Division at the United Nations. He somehow succeeded in having fact-gathering and scientific analysis accepted as major functions of the Division. He fostered within the Division the standards of preciseness and objectivity that he tried to maintain at the Office of Population Research. Partly as the result of the impetus he gave to the Division, some of the world's leading demographers have served with it, and it has made discoveries and enriched the literature with some of the most important contributions of the period since it was founded.

The Population Council cannot be counted as Notestein's creation, but its functions and strategy were planned at an organizing conference in which his ideas were critically important. The council began operation in 1952, when John D. Rockefeller, 3rd, supplied its initial funding and became its first president. It was a small organization, limited at first to modest support of demographic research, to biomedical research on human reproduction, and to providing fellowships for advanced training both in demography and the biomedical field, primarily to candidates from less developed countries. The next president of the council was Frederick Osborn, the person already described as the prime mover in initiating the Office of Population Research. When Osborn retired in 1959, Notestein succeeded him as president of the Council.

Notestein came to the Population Council at an opportune moment. In its early years most of its funds were personal contributions by John Rockefeller, but by 1959 it was receiving support from the Ford and Rockefeller Foundations. In 1959, and for the first few years of Notestein's presidency of the council, the United States Government and the United Nations were still barred from technical assistance in family planning, and the Population Council was the only organization in the world from which countries could ask for help. Under these conditions and with Notestein's leadership, the Population Council became a critical component in the expansion of technical assistance; in the extension of training both in demography and the biomedical aspects of reproduction; and in the development of these two scientific fields. It was of great assistance in launching family planning programs in South Korea, Taiwan, and many other countries. It set up systems of continuing evaluation of these programs that were invaluable for their effectiveness, and have been useful models for others. The biomedical research program at the Council provided intellectual leadership in an area that in 1959 had few resources in money, or personnel. Now that financial support is on a much larger scale, and many laboratories are working in the field, the Council program is still influential. An instance of the practical impact of this program is its funding (about 95 percent) of the development of the intrauterine contraceptive device. In 20 years the cumulative number of Population Council Fellows reached about 1,400, of whom some 1,150 were from Asia, Africa, and Latin America. A substantial fraction of the professional demographers in the less developed countries are P.C. fellows. Other, larger programs financed by governments are building on the foundations established by the Population Council.

Notestein's was an unusual personality. A large man—he seemed a little reserved and imposing when first met—but soon proved himself a warm, loyal, and generous friend. He had more concern for his colleagues and employees than some of them suspected. His written work is a model of lucidity and graceful expression, but it was composed in the world's most illegible hand. He sometimes had to ask his secretary to decipher passages he had written in the manuscript he was working on. His students could not read the incisive comments he had written on their papers. Once when a Japanese graduate student had made a presentation in a seminar at Princeton, Notestein outlined some comments on the blackboard. George Barclay remarked that apparently Notestein had felt compelled to write in Japanese.

Notestein's informal speech, including his class teaching, was delivered in a rather clipped cadence, and was full of unusual figures of speech that baffled his foreign students and doubtless the diplomats at the United Nations. Yet on more formal occasions, whether giving a prepared statement, or being called upon to comment, he spoke with great precision and clarity, and frequently with eloquence.

Notestein's skeptical temperament sometimes led him to be iconoclastic. Thus, when a younger friend was elected to the American Philosophical Society, he congratulated him warmly, and then added "You'll enjoy being a member; it is a pleasant and harmless mutual admiration society." Although his background was rigorously Presbyterian, his natural outlook made him agnostic. At his funeral the minister (a relative by marriage) said that he received a letter from Notestein a few months earlier, saying that should the minister be called on to officiate at such a ceremony, he was to announce that Notestein had not been a member of any organized church. Honesty and consistency were his hallmark, even after his life was over.

V

$\mathcal{R}$ESEARCH ASSISTANT AT THE OPR TO OFFICER IN THE NAVY

IN MAY OF 1941, after two years of graduate courses, I took the so-called general examinations for the PhD in economics. At Princeton successful completion of both written and oral exams in five fields within the candidate's department is one of the requirements for the doctorate; another is the completion of an acceptable dissertation, followed by a final oral exam. I passed the preliminary examinations, and normally, I would have begun work on a thesis. At the time, however, the war in Europe was intense, and the U.S. had initiated its selective service program to be prepared for possible involvement. I had been issued a very low draft number and faced early induction into the military; I chose not to begin work on a thesis, since its early interruption would be inevitable.

At the same time, the Economic, Financial, and Transit Department of the League of Nations, which had moved temporarily to Princeton from Geneva, arranged with Princeton University for the Office of Population Research to undertake a study of the future population of Europe and the Soviet Union, to provide information that might be useful in any postwar peace settlements. Notestein offered me a job as a research assistant while I was waiting for my induction notice. My assignment was to develop suitable methods of population projection, and to supervise the collection of the necessary data and the projections themselves. The results were projected populations of 28 European countries and the Soviet Union, at 5-year time intervals from 1940 to 1970. The projected populations were classified by sex and 5-year age groups. It was necessary to develop uniform methods for estimating the future course of fertility and mortality in all of the national populations, and in some instances to adjust for errors in the pre-war data. The projections deliberately made no estimates of the effect of the war on fertility and mortality, on the assumption that these effects could be incorporated after the return of peace, when the requisite information might be available.

In the fall, Sue and I decided to get married without waiting to see what would happen when I was called into service. The marriage took place in October at the Presbyterian church in Plainfield, where Sue's parents then lived. My father officiated at the service; Sue's sister Holly was maid of honor, my brother Jim was best man, my classmates Johnny Matthews and Walter Daub were ushers.

Frank Lorimer had been given a visiting appointment at the OPR to undertake a large separate study of the population of the Soviet Union. Frank was on the faculty at American University in Washington; during his work on the Russian study, he made frequent visits to Princeton. In my analysis of some of the populations of Eastern Europe, I had found it necessary to adjust the mortality data from before the war for understatement of death rates at older ages. It was clear that similar adjustments were needed for the Soviet Union, and during Frank's visits we worked it out. Shortly before our wedding he wrote to ask whether I would come to Washington to explain the procedure to his graduate students. I told him that I would be glad to accept, but might still be on a honeymoon. Frank sent a telegram saying "Please come and bring the new Coale to our castle."

In the fall of 1941, I had received a form sponsored by several Washington agencies, called a roster of scientific and specialized personnel. After Pearl Harbor, having received an induction notice from my draft board, I drove immediately to Washington, and went to the first organization on the letter head of the "Roster." It was the National Academy of Sciences, which was unknown to me at the time. I walked into the office of the president of the Academy, and explained that I believed that I could better serve the war effort, following the spirit of the roster, by doing something using the advanced courses in statistics I had taken rather than undergoing basic training for the infantry. He said that the Academy was involved only in the natural sciences, and I told him of the courses I had taken in math and physics. He had been a professor of physics at Princeton and knew of the courses I mentioned. He asked me if I knew anything about radio, and I replied that I had made short wave sets as a hobby when I was in high school. Then he inquired if I thought I could handle a course in radio engineering, and I said I was sure I could. He picked up the phone and called the Navy Department across Constitution Avenue, and gave me the name of the officer I should see. The officer offered me on the spot a commission as an ensign in the naval reserve, and said I would soon receive orders to go to a pre-radar course in radio engineering, and would then go through the training program in radar operated for military officers at MIT.

While I had taken relevant courses such as functions of complex variables, I had never formally studied electricity. Back in Princeton waiting for my orders, I enrolled at the beginning of the second semester in the introductory course in radio engineering, which began with a review of alternating electrical currents. After a week or two of this course, I received my orders: report to Fort Schuyler on March 1 for an orientation course in Navy rules and traditions, then on April 1 to Bowdoin for a three month program in pre-radar radio engineering. I wrote to the office that issued the orders, stating that I believed that I would spend my time more efficiently continuing the introductory course at Princeton rather than going to Fort Schuyler. In response came a letter commending my desire to be more efficient, and issuing new orders: to report on March 1 to the Harvard pre-radar radio engineering program. This proved to be a very intensive program with five days a week of morning lectures and afternoon laboratories.

At the end of May, 1942, I completed the course in radio engineering at Harvard and progressed into the three month program in radar conducted by MIT. The program was not held on the MIT campus in Cambridge, but on the top floor of a commercial building on Atlantic Avenue, overlooking the Boston harbor. The radar school took over both the top floor and the roof of the Harbor Building. Laboratory benches and lecture rooms were inside; outside on the roof were the antennas of operating radar sets.

The students in this school were officers in the Army, Navy, and Air Corps. The three month program began with two months of work on the components of radar sets such as modulators, transmitters, wave guides and transmission lines, receivers, and antennas. In these two months lectures were given on components; the students also spent several hours at laboratory benches working with prototypes. In the third month, actual radar sets were the subject of study, again both in lectures and laboratory. Each month a new class was admitted; the three one-month segments operated simultaneously. I did well in the radar school, and when the three months of training ended by the first of September, I was retained to teach in the program, first, in the laboratory of months one and two. I was later shifted to lecturing in the third month, on actual Navy radar sets.

Of course unfamiliar radar sets were constantly being developed and introduced into use. The graduates of the radar school went to naval bases and large vessels to supervise the installation, operation, and maintenance of this new equipment. When a new model of radar came out, we had to get one or two sets for the lab. Working with the manufacturer's circuit diagrams, we had to devise instructional drawings so that the operation of the set would be understandable. It was a challenging responsibility.

The teaching staff was drawn from the MIT faculty, plus young civilian experts that MIT had hired, and military officers who had done well in the program. An amusing episode involved a civilian on the staff of the school, Joe Kline, who was drafted into the Navy. The system worked well enough to assign him as a naval officer to the MIT radar program without the pre-radar radio engineering. When he arrived in the third-month laboratory, he presented a challenge for his alleged teachers. Many of the third-month lab exercises consisted of finding faults in a radar set, faults which had been deliberately planted by the staff. One day Joe Kline's lab exercise involved an anti-aircraft fire control radar. His instructor conceived the idea of pointing the antenna (which was out on the roof) straight up in the air, so that there would not be the usual echos from ships in the harbor, from other buildings, etc. Joe turned on the set, looked at the screen, and said "The antenna must be directed straight up."

During my period of teaching (about twenty hours of lectures a week when I was assigned to the third month of the program), I came to be more expert in electronics than in the social sciences. The staff of the school put together a book on "Principles of Radar," and I wrote a section on automatic frequency control. Another professional adventure that I had while at the school was the result of a decision in the Navy Department that the teachers should have some field experience. Feeling somewhat guilty about having escaped the risks of the war, I requested assignment on a destroyer that would accompany a convoy to North Africa, where American troops were in combat.

The Bureau of Personnel disappointed this romantic request by sending me for one week's duty in radar repair at the Brooklyn Navy Yard, and three week's duty at the headquarters of Atlantic Fleet destroyers, at Casco Bay, near Portland, Maine. At Brooklyn I saw some of the practical problems of maintenance, and at Casco Bay I went on short training voyages on a different destroyer each trip. On each voyage I would give some informal instruction to the radar technicians, and observe how anti–aircraft radar worked at sea against overflying planes, and generally learned something about real conditions. For example, one of the destroyers returned into the Bay in a dense fog, and I helped pick up each successive invisible navigational buoy, and even a floating oil can.

After three years on the staff of the radar school, I was transferred to the Navy liaison office at the Radiation Laboratory, also operated by MIT. The Radiation Lab was the principal center for basic research in the development of improved radar, and was the major source of many of the improvements that occurred during the war. Its scientific personnel included a number of outstanding physicists, some of whom later won Nobel prizes. The physicists' application of old basic science (one of them remarked that most of the science underlying radar was more than 40 years old) served them better in coming up with important inventions than did the preoccupation of radio engineers with problems in radio transmission and reception of the 1940s.

There were eight or ten Navy officers in the Liaison Office, under the leadership of Commander Ferrier, an Annapolis graduate. My assignment was to facilitate relations between the radar section of the Bureau of Ships and the work in the Lab in developing ship-borne radar equipment. Most of my time was spent in Cambridge, but I made a trip to the Navy Department in Washington about twice a month.

An example of the awkward position I sometimes felt I was occupying as a liaison officer arose when the damage done to the Pacific fleet from Japanese Kamakazi pilots increased alarmingly. The Kamakazis were suicidal dive bombers who managed to get nearly overhead above naval vessels and then dove a plane loaded with explosives directly into a ship. The radars that traced enemy air craft had a search beam with a maximum elevation of something less than 45 degrees, so that when a plane was overhead it was not visible on this equipment. The RadLab scientists came up with a proposed design of equipment for high elevation searching, to be mounted high above deck. The Navy experts demurred, saying that existing radar and other heavy gear installed at high levels already threatened the stability of ships, and that the new equipment would have to be low in installation and light in weight. The scientists would have preferred to be presented with the overall strategic problem, with a description of existing shipboard equipment, and then asked to come up with the best solution, including the relocation of existing gear. I sympathized with the laboratory attitude, and felt, as I often did, more a representative of the RadLab scientists than of the Bureau of Ships.

Personal Life while in the Navy

After our wedding on October 18, 1941, Sue and I moved into a one–room apartment in a university building in Princeton not far from the campus. When the March first date of reporting at Harvard (in my naval reserve orders) approached, I went up to Cambridge in search of a place to live. On Sumner Road, near the Harvard Yard, Mrs. Coyle operated a house with rooms she rented to students. The house contained two small apartments, one on the first floor that bordered the porch, and the other in the basement under the first floor apartment.

The basement apartment was occupied by a young couple, Robert and Jeanette Galambos. Bob was a young experimental biologist who with a colleague had just discovered that bats navigate by the equivalent of sonar: they emit a series of squeaks at a pitch higher than the audible range for humans. Detecting the time and the direction of the echo reflected from an obstacle or an insect, the bat can avoid collisions and catch prey.

The Galamboses were scheduled for the birth of a child, and were moving into a nearby larger apartment. Mrs. Coyle showed me the basement apartment, with the warning that there were lots of mops on the wall; "mops," I found, was Irish for maps. A short time later, Sue came to Cambridge and we moved into Mrs. Coyle's basement apartment.

The appointment (beginning on September 1st) as an instructor in the MIT radar program was especially welcome because Sue was eight months pregnant. Our first child was born in the Boston Lying-in Hospital on September 22, 1942. After I took Sue to the hospital, I accepted an invitation to have supper with the Galamboses. These experienced parents dissuaded me from telephoning to check on the birth, saying that nothing would happen for hours. I finally insisted on phoning, and was connected with the delivery room, where an impatient doctor said "Where have you been? You are the father of a seven and a half pound boy!"

Sue wanted to name the child after me, but I objected that Ansley had been a difficult name about which I had been teased when I was a child. For example, I was called "Ann." I agreed to name the boy Ansley with the proviso that we would call him "Pete" while he was young, in imitation of my friend Earle Blair Fox who had insisted on "Pete Fox." The irony is that when the child entered school he insisted on being called Ansley.

When Pete was born, we moved upstairs into the more comfortable first floor apartment in Mrs. Coyle's house, and a year or so later into half a three storey double house on Bartlett Avenue in Arlington. The larger quarters of the house were more agreeable, but the trip to the Radar School in downtown Boston was much longer, and Sue was more isolated. During our first year in Arlington, our younger son was born, on June 1, 1944. I received a call from Sue while at work in which she reported premonitory pains. I hurried home, phoned the hospital, got Sue into the car and rushed away. She was experiencing frequent contractions and severe pain. Our car was a Mercury convertible that had belonged to Sue's mother, and had been given to Sue as a wedding present. We sped through the streets of Cambridge and Boston, going through red lights with horn blowing. The irony was that the noisy car was a convertible with the top down driven by a young Naval officer accompanied by a pretty young woman. I kept hoping we would be pulled over by a traffic policeman, so we could acquire an escort. We did reach the Lying-in Hospital; Sue was rolled inside in a wheel chair, and delivered the baby in about half an hour.

The next year was difficult for the new mother. No adequate help could be hired; and the new baby (christened Robert Campbell Coale in honor of his maternal grandfather) had chronic indigestion and cried a great deal. Brother Pete, experiencing unavoidable neglect, developed acute sibling envy. On weekdays I could not escape my Naval duty to provide badly needed paternal help. The fine pediatrician who treated the baby summarized his troubled first year: "Rob has had trouble deciding whether he wants to stay around."

Pete's sibling envy remained acute. He had been a very cheerful, well behaved, and precocious infant before the birth of his brother. His jealous behavior reached a potentially dangerous extreme. When Rob was about a year old, the two had been playing in the back yard together for a few minutes when I noticed some tan fragments falling from Rob's mouth. Pete had fed him a raw mushroom; he asked "Will he turn green and die?" (From Babar the Elephant). We rushed to the hospital in Cambridge, where an intern pumped out the child's stomach. It was Sunday afternoon; we went to the Biology building on the Harvard campus; I was asking the guard how I might phone a botanist when a professor came in the door. I told him the problem, and showed him the mushroom, which I had brought along. He phoned a botanist colleague, and then performed the most reassuring gesture imaginable: he ate the fragment of mushroom.

$\mathcal{R}$ETURN TO CIVILIAN LIFE

As PEACE ARRIVED with the surrender of both Germany and Japan, I decided to return to academia by looking for a dissertation topic (probably a demographic subject) and considering where I might do the research. There was an associated problem of income; with a wife and two infant children, I could not subsist on the usual graduate fellowship, assuming one were offered to me. After the official end of the war, while still nominally on active duty and then while on terminal leave, I sat in on a course at Harvard in quantum mechanics, and in two graduate seminars in economics. Before I had made definite plans for a dissertation, the Social Science Research Council offered me an opportunity that seemed especially designed for my needs. It was called a demobilization award, and called for a continuation of the military salary of a young officer with dependents who was far along toward an advanced degree and could not subsist on a graduate students stipend. Of course I joyfully took advantage of this award.

Before I could decide on the best place to live (stay in Arlington or move to Princeton), the SSRC offered me a salaried position as the secretary of a committee it was creating on the social implications of atomic energy. I could continue in residence in Arlington, and come to New York for meetings and consultation. The Demobilization Award would be held for me while I served as secretary of the committee. It was an opportunity I did not resist. The chairman of the committee was Winfield Riefler, an economist at the Institute for Advanced Study in Princeton, and its members included two prominent physicists, a political scientist who specialized in international affairs, a sociologist and a demographer. The Committee sponsored research on such social science topics as the economics of producing electrical power from nuclear fission, and the prospects for international restriction of atomic weapons.

The members of the committee recognized another area in which there might be social problems associated with atomic energy, but could not formulate a feasible research strategy that would suit a committee-sponsored project. The area in question was the reaction of nations to the threat of this unprecedentedly lethal weapon. The committee resolved this dilemma by asking its secretary to examine the problems associated with vulnerability to atomic weapons, and to report the results of this examination to the committee.

I responded to the committee's request by preparing a written statement concerning the problems of reducing vulnerability, a statement that came to occupy 115 printed pages. The committee commented on the draft at various stages in its preparation. When it was finished, it was published as a book by the Princeton University Press. The strength of the preoccupation with atomic weapons at the time is indicated by the book's being reviewed in the Sunday *New York Times.*

When the work with the committee finished, I turned my attention to writing a PhD dissertation. The economics department had long accepted dissertations on noneconomic topics, provided that they incorporated social science of sufficient quality. (For example, "The mean age at marriage in India as ascertained from census data," and "The projection of national populations: a report on the state of an art"). I wondered whether a study of vulnerability would qualify as a topic. When I suggested this possibility to the professor in charge of graduate work in economics, I mentioned that by rule a dissertation should be publishable. Was a dissertation that had already been published eligible? The committee responsible for the decision allowed me to offer the book as a thesis provided I wrote an additional and more empirical chapter applying to a specific industry the principles I had proposed for making a strategic industry less vulnerable. I wrote such a chapter on making the availability of aluminum less vulnerable, and incorporated it into the text in a rather complicated way. I had not retained a typescript of the book, so I bought two copies, cut off the spines with a heavy paper cutter, and pasted each page to a sheet of letter size paper. I then combined these pages with the typewritten new chapter. When I was pasting the printed pages to typewriter paper in a reading room in the library, a fellow graduate student remarked: "I see you are writing your thesis."

I had one further adventure before receiving the doctorate. The chairman of my final oral exam, Frank Graham, said that the tradition for the oral was to ask the candidate questions only about his dissertation. (The so-called final defense). He had checked the written rules, however, and they stipulated that the questions could deal with anything in the discipline, whether or not related to the thesis. I had made essentially no preparation for the defense, believing that my examiners could scarcely have given a fraction of the thought that I had to vulnerability. Graham said that the written rules would be followed rather than the tradition of a defense of the dissertation. Not having studied economics for about six years, I would have been in an utter panic if I had been told this decision before. But on the spur of the moment, my subconscious functioned well, and I was not humiliated.

VII

$\mathcal{I}$NTELLECTUAL DETOURS
1947 – 1953

IN THE FALL OF 1947 I was appointed an assistant professor in economics at Princeton. For several ensuing years my research was stimulated by opportunities arising more from unusual qualifications I had gained than from strong intellectual curiosity. It was this experience that has led me to advise students to study subjects in which they have a strong interest rather than those that will provide career advantages.

In 1948 a grant was offered jointly by the Social Science Research Council and the National Research Council to support the study of natural sciences by a professional social scientist, or *vice versa*. I felt at nearly a professional level in both broad areas. Instead of seeking to study physical or social science, I requested support to spend two years analyzing the economic effects of technological change and the relations between science and technology. I also applied for temporary membership in the Institute for Advanced Study in Princeton as the locale of my proposed research. Both requests were granted.

The Institute was founded with financial support from the Bamberger family to provide an environment in which intellectuals could carry out research free of the demands of teaching and administration. A number of outstanding intellectuals were permanent members of the Institute faculty; the majority of the residents were temporary members, given use of the facilities at the Institute, but with their own financial support. I was given a small office, use of the library, and informal access to highly–distinguished permanent members.

Among my most pleasant memories of these two years were the daily lunches in the cafeteria on the top floor of the main building. Mathematicians and physicists strongly outnumbered all other disciplines combined, and their scientific conversation at lunch seemed quite esoteric to non-scientists. A custom developed: the historians, classicists, literary persons, economists, and others who were not mathematicians or physicists, ate together at a large round table. After my first few weeks at the Institute, I invited my wife to join me for lunch in the cafeteria. I did not feel that I should have her sit at the round table, so we took a table for two. A man with a distinguished and familiar profile passed with his tray on his way to the round table. "Isn't that T.S. Eliot?" asked Sue. I said that I did not believe so. Eliot had been at the table for about a week, and judging from his accent and his knowledge of English affairs, I thought he was a British economist.

One day at lunch a somewhat stuffy senior member was discussing the Middle East, and mentioned a Sheikh he had met. He pronounced the word "shake" and a colleague asked, "What did you say?" "Shake." "How's that?" "Shake." "What?" "Sheek!" "I knew you could say it!" said the colleague.

On another occasion there was very gloomy talk about the adverse changes in conditions and prospects in England: war damage to physical facilities, loss of life among its most talented young men, shift from a leading creditor to a huge debtor, etc. A young man who was working as a research assistant for a senior historian burst out: "There must be some solution to this problem!" Walter Stewart softly replied: "Young man, it's not true that every problem has a solution, but only that every situation has an outcome."

I established very rewarding friendships at the Institute: with Walter Stewart, a senior economist; with Harold Cherniss, a Classics scholar and specialist on Plato, and with the Director, the physicist Robert Oppenheimer. My friendship with Cherniss was especially close and lasted until his death long after I had left the Institute. When the 1952 presidential election was approaching, Harold told me that contrary to the polls, he felt that Stevenson had a good chance to win. He said that his insight was partially the result of his undergraduate education when he had majored in political science because there were few scholarships for a classicist. With this background he had noted that if Stevenson carried every state that had been carried by the Democrats since 1936 (and one more), he would win. The night following the election Harold and Ruth came to our house for dinner. He said that he owed us an apology, and I replied that no apology was owed for a wrong prediction. No, he said, I should apologize because I forgot my master. He then noted that Plato had expressed his reservations about elections by popular vote by saying: imagine a civil trial between a pastry cook and a philosopher before a jury of children.

Overall, I had an enjoyable time at the Institute, not lacking in intellectual stimulus. My research plan, to study the effects of technological change on the economy and on the measurement of real income and the average level of prices, was not a success. I did not have an exciting original idea that I wanted to explore, but thought that I had what economists call a comparative advantage. I thought that I could describe the sequence of Edison's discovery of the emission of free electrons from a heated filament (a scientific discovery in the midst of technological research), followed by the technical application of this discovery to the development of vacuum tubes and electronic amplifiers, followed by the incorporation of electronic amplifiers in equipment used in basic science, such as cyclotrons. I showed a manuscript analyzing such interrelations to Oppenheimer; he read it through, gave it back, and said: "This is right."

In short, I worked hard at the Institute, but the manuscripts I wrote, although competent, were uninspired.

After leaving the Institute for Advanced Study, I became involved in research on military questions, largely because I had been author of the book on vulnerability. I was offered work as a consultant to the Weapons Systems Evaluation Group at the Pentagon, and went to Washington two or three times a month on this mission. When the RAND Corporation was established to conduct basic research for the Air Force, I was again asked to participate and spent two full summers in Santa Monica as part of RAND's economic division. At WSEG and my first summer at RAND, my work was to help develop principles for the selection of targets in atomic warfare: how to balance the number of weapons against the force of individual bombs in developing an arsenal, considering the area of effectiveness against different types of targets, etc. In my second summer at RAND, another consultant (Harold Barnett) and I were asked to advise the management whether RAND should accept a separate large contract with the Air Force to take responsibility for Air Force logistics. We concluded that it would be a misuse of RAND resources to take over inventory management and bookkeeping, but if logistics were flexibly enough defined, there was a potential role for RAND. The flexible definition we had in mind was logistics as a strategy for insuring that essential air force functions could always be provided. For example, we suggested that to insure that the air force could operate in Europe in the event of war, spare planes and other equipment might be maintained ready to move at diverse places in the United States and elsewhere. In the event of an attack on an airbase, the wreckage would be bulldozed from the field and replacement planes and spare parts flown in (as planned) from distant centers. Consideration of such alternatives would fit the nature of RAND better than being asked to keep track of the inventory of air force possessions.

The consequence of this somewhat aimless research track on technological change at the Institute and as a consultant on military matters was that when I was finishing my sixth year as an assistant professor, the Economics Faculty recommended my appointment as a tenured associate professor, but the interdepartmental committee charged with the final decision rejected the recommendation. The rule at Princeton for assistant professors is "up or out"; the maximum term of service without tenure is six years. This rule avoids exploitation of non–promotable junior faculty to provide low–cost teaching. In short, I was offered a seventh but terminal year. This news came when I was spending my second summer at RAND. I was immediately offered a permanent job there at a handsome salary. I responded that before accepting a permanent position at RAND I wanted to establish a firm intellectual non-military academic base to which I might later return. I asked Frank Notestein if during my terminal year I might serve as a research associate at the Office of Population Research. Thus I returned to demography. I have come to realize I should have returned in 1947. These six years starting when I was just 30 could have been among my most productive rather than ending in a veto of the recommendation for my promotion.

VIII

THE STUDY OF POPULATION CHANGE AND ECONOMIC DEVELOPMENT IN LOW INCOME COUNTRIES

A MAJOR PROJECT with which I became involved when I returned to the OPR in the 1950s was a study of the relation of population change to economic progress in less developed countries. This project began as a reaction to a request to Notestein from Eugene Black, who was president of the World Bank. Black wanted Frank to write an essay explaining the importance of slower growth of population in helping economic progress in the poorer countries. Notestein responded that there was not enough soundly established knowledge of the topic, and that much substantive research was needed. The ensuing discussion led to an agreement that the Bank would support a project at the OPR, in which I would serve as the principal demographic researcher and that we would find a suitable experienced economist to work with me. (In my first year back at the OPR launching this and other projects, my promotion to associate professor was approved, and I was appointed assistant director of the Office.)

When I was starting on this study of the relation of population change to economic development, and needed a productive economic expert as a collaborator, my first idea was Harold Barnett, with whom I had worked in the summer of 1953 at RAND. He was later involved with Resources for the Future. He was quite attracted by the idea of working on our project, but felt his commitments would not permit him to do so. He suggested we approach Edgar M. Hoover, who was well known for his book on the location of industry and his contributions to several other economic subjects. Hoover had been appointed to the president's Council of Economic Advisors, but he found our project fascinating, and also was eager to escape his work at the Council, which was subject to security classification. We intended to appoint him as a senior research staff member at the OPR, with the rank of professor. In spite of the fact that Hoover's pay was covered by the financial support of the World Bank, the highest salary that the University would approve (about the same as Notestein's) was substantially less than what Ed was then receiving; he reluctantly turned the offer down. I called Barnett with this news, and he responded with a remarkable combination of insight and friendship. He phoned Hoover and said: "Ed, you don't know your own mind. You don't care about money. Here is an opportunity to move out of your intellectual dead end into work that you will love, with stimulating collaborators, on a question of the greatest importance." Hoover thought it over, realized that Harold was right, and accepted the job.

Thus began what I view as a fruitful and extremely rewarding collaboration. The International Bank gave Ed an office and secretarial help in its Washington headquarters. We visited one another in Washington or Princeton often to supplement our frequent exchange of manuscript drafts and memos. At the time we were starting this project (as today), there were two strongly held opposing views about the effects of rapid population growth on successful economic progress in less developed countries. One school held that continued rapid growth even for a few years could have calamitous effects, since these countries were already overpopulated. The other school denied any adverse effects of population growth and said that poverty in the less developed areas had other origins: for example exploitative colonial administration. According to this school, the measures needed were a redistribution of income, an effective economic plan, government ownership of the means of production, or other nondemographic programs. Population policy was considered irrelevant by members of this school. We decided to avoid either of these positions. We did not try to show that a high birth rate was catastrophic, nor that it was no problem at all.

Our plan was to determine what difference it would make in a specific country if the then current high rate of childbearing were to continue for 30 years, or alternatively were to be reduced by 50 percent over this period. We planned to begin by making numerical projections of the population classified by age and sex, under each of the two sets of assumptions. We intended to then incorporate the alternative projected populations into an appropriate model of the growth of the economy.

The country we chose to examine first was India. I undertook projections of the Indian population; and Ed took principal responsibility for the economic calculations. At all stages in every phase of the planning, the calculations, and the composition of the text, the work was fully collaborative. Our work began in Princeton and Washington using information on India available in this country. I used stable population analysis and other features of the technical demography I had mastered to adjust the Indian population listed in the 1951 census for errors, to estimate the fertility and mortality schedules to which the population was subject, and to project the future course of mortality until the 1980s. (Future fertility was based on our alternative assumptions of no change and a 50 percent reduction). I shared these preliminary projections with Hoover for him to use in his preliminary economic analysis.

It became apparent that we needed to visit India to talk to Indian experts and see for ourselves some of the evidence we needed.

A Visit to India for the Coale-Hoover Project

In the fall of 1955 Sue and I, and Ed and Mary Hoover, went to India to advance our research on the relation of population change to economic progress. In India we made our residential headquarters at a hotel in New Delhi, where the Asian representative of the Rockefeller Foundation, Dr. Marshall Balfour, had an apartment and an office. Balfour was an indispensable help. The Rockefeller Foundation had played an essential role in promoting the development of medicine and public health in India. Most of the health officials we met in India had studied at Harvard or Johns Hopkins, or in London, with Rockefeller fellowships. As I traveled to many of the states in India to get first-hand information about disease control and mortality (registration of vital events was not trustworthy), Balfour would telephone the minister of health in the state (generally a former Rockefeller Fellow) who would meet us at the airport and later introduce me to the appropriate local persons.

An unforgettable adventure with a local medical authority occurred in Madras State, at the Community Development Public Health Training Center in Poonamallee. We had spent several days in Madras city speaking to different authorities both medical and economic, and I had asked to go to Poonamallee, because I had heard that one of the officials there had especially robust data on infant mortality, the most elusive variable to nail down. I went to Poonamallee and found the recommended official. As it turned out, he had no especially valid information about infant mortality, but he invited me to lunch at his cottage. With our fingers we ate boiled rice served on a palm leaf. He asked me if I would go with him after lunch to his class of community health worker trainees. On the way to the classroom he asked if he could introduce me to his class. I agreed, and after leading me to the front of the room full of perhaps 30 students, he said that a professor visiting from America was going to speak to them about the use of statistics in rural public health work in India. I gulped and then launched into a half hour discourse on the subject, calling attention to my observation in my visits to community centers that health officials tended to record only such data as the number of yards of drainage ditches that had been installed. I suggested that the health programs should include frequent calls to get information on individual households and collect such data as deaths and illness of individuals classified by age and sex.

A particularly interesting contribution to my insight into the demography of India was a visit Sue and I made to a public health project in North India near Ludhiana. Known as the Khanna project (the village of Khanna was the headquarters), the study was an attempt to introduce contraception to the native population in conjunction with the initiation of rudimentary public health measures. It was an adaptation of a classic epidemiological design in which experimental villages were offered information and supplies for the practice of contraception in conjunction with health services, and control villages were provided only the latter. The project was in its very early stages, so we saw no results, but we did have an intimate introduction to village life in walking tours with the resident director, John Wyon, and his wife Elizabeth. Both had lived in India and were fluent in the local dialect. Sue was escorted through the village by Elizabeth, and I, by John. Sue met the women, and I the men, with interesting translations of any questions. The intense segregation of the sexes in Northern India is illustrated by the fact that during our contemporaneous tours of a village we never glimpsed the other party made up of the other sex.

As we had hoped, Hoover and I developed a solid basis for our study during our visit to India. In the preface to our book based on this research, we named 70 persons in India who had given us notable help, including the secretary of the planning commission, professors at academic institutions, and directors of development and health projects in diverse regions of the country. When we returned to America, we resumed our collaborative work, and in the summer of 1956 mailed out a preliminary draft manuscript on the results of our work on India to various experts for a preliminary reaction. The key conclusion we had reached was that there would be a substantial increase in income per adult consumer with no change in fertility, but an increase about 40 percent greater if the rate of childbearing were to fall by 50 percent in 25 years. I remember a reaction of Simon Kuznets to this result when he saw the preliminary draft: "An extra advantage of 40 percent in income per consumer in 30 years is not much, about 1 percent per year, compounded. I can readily imagine various economic programs that would increase income by 1 percent annually." In fact our conclusion indicated significant prospective economic progress even with continued high fertility, and significant if somewhat modest additional progress should fertility be substantially reduced in the next generation.

Our next step was to make a similar but less intense analysis of the economic outcome of alternative fertility trends in another less developed country. We chose Mexico as this second case because it shared with India a sustained level of high fertility, but differed from India in size of its population, and in the then current levels of development and mortality. Again I made projections of the population, and Ed estimated how the economy would develop given the two alternative demographic courses.

In the fall of 1956 we paid a visit to Mexico and sought, as in India, to get expert local guidance on the Mexican population and economy. The results of our analysis of the prospects in Mexico were incorporated in "Population Growth and Economic Development in Low Income Countries" completed in 1957 and published in 1958.

The Outcome of the Coale-Hoover Study of Population and Development

The Coale-Hoover project has been the subject of much discussion; but the conclusions have sometimes been misunderstood. I shall offer a few words about its results as seen nearly 40 years later. Our strategy had been to make two population projections for each of two low–income countries which, as of the 1950s, had experienced no consequential decline in fertility: in each country one projection was made with continued high fertility, and the other on the assumption of a 50 percent decline in 25 years. We then tried to estimate the evolution of the economy in these two projected populations to determine how much economic difference a large reduction in fertility would make.

We concluded that the population with reduced fertility would after 30 years enjoy an income per equivalent adult consumer (children under 15 counted as one half of adult consumers) about 40 percent larger than a population in which fertility did not decline. This result cannot be empirically verified, because only one fertility trajectory is followed in each population. But in both India and Mexico there was little decline in fertility before 1970, and I have compared the actual change in population in India until the mid 1970s with the no-change-in-fertility projection. The population was projected to increase by 49 percent above 1951 by 1971 and by 91 percent by 1981. The 1971 and 1981 censuses showed increases of 52 and 89 percent. Birth rates, death rates, and age composition also followed closely the no-change-in-fertility projection. Hoover estimated that GNP at constant prices would increase by 95 percent with constant fertility; the official estimate is an increase of 103 percent. (When I told Ed how close his projected GNP figure was, he said "Blind luck.") This close match of the projected population and GNP on the assumption of no change in fertility to the actual figures does not of course prove that our estimate of the extra income per consumer realizable with reduced fertility was correct. That both the projected and the recorded GNP per consumer rose by more than 25 percent in 20 years with continued high fertility is counter to the doomsday sentiments expressed by some analysts in the 1950s.

In Mexico, the population was multiplied by 2.03 from 1955 to 1975; our projection with no change in fertility gave a multiplier of 1.93. The projected crude birth and death rates with no change in fertility (with constant fertility) were very close to the official figures until after 1970 when a fertility decline began. Some of the actual social and economic changes were surprisingly favorable, despite the continued high level of childbearing. The income per capita rose by 89 percent from 1955 to 1975; the number of children attending school was multiplied by 3.56 from 1950 to 1970. Do these indications of rapid progress contradict our conclusions about greater gains with a reduction in fertility? Not in my opinion. Our aim was to compare progress with and without a reduction in the rate of childbearing, and there is no record of what would have happened had fertility been reduced by one half. By our reasoning income per equivalent adult consumer would have been some 30–50 percent higher. One might ask: how would it have been possible to do better than multiplying school enrollment by 3.56? Actually with continued high fertility there were more children not in school in 1970 than in 1950. Had fertility fallen, 100 percent enrollment could have been achieved, probably with fewer resources than were actually employed.

*F*AMILY LIFE AFTER WWII

WHEN I HAD FINISHED MY WORK for the SSRC and accepted an appointment as assistant professor of economics at Princeton University, Sue and I and the two children moved to New Jersey. The only place we could find to live in this early postwar period was in temporary housing that had been constructed for veterans: married graduate students or junior faculty. The buildings were assembled from army barracks that had been torn down and moved onto what had once been polo fields. The cottages were small and primitive, and widely known as the "barracks" or the "project." Our new home had a tiny living room connected (with no door) to a tiny kitchen, with a small bath (no tub, shower only), and two very small bedrooms. For the boys, we put double-deck bunks in the smaller of the two bedrooms, and twin beds for Sue and me in the other. Heating was provided by a kerosene stove; the fuel was stored in a tank outside the back door and had to be hand carried inside and poured into the small tank attached to the stove that provided central heating. My first task was to run copper tubing along the empty space under the floor to provide gravity feed from the outdoor tank directly to the stove. The refrigerator was not electric, but was supplied with ice bought from a delivery wagon. There was almost no storage space; the children's tricycles and wagons were kept outside the front door.

A high point of our stay in the barracks was our adoption of a dog. Buck was a large crossbreed, mostly collie, who was living in the neighborhood without any apparent owner. We heard that a naval officer who had taught in the training program at Princeton during the war had left the dog when ordered to a new station, and that Buck had then been fed by naval cadets until the training program ended. He then simply stayed in the project living on handouts. He appeared on the back steps outside our kitchen door, wagged his tail and salivated. He was too dignified to whine or scratch. We soon supplemented our scraps with purchased dog food, and Buck adopted us. He was a very loyal and affectionate pet; when our two young boys were playing outside in the vacant land near our cottage, he would lie down facing them and keep an eye on their activities. Early one morning we were wakened by boisterous barking from a pack of dogs who were pestering a herd of superannuated army horses that a colonel in the ROTC program maintained in an empty field behind us. I went to the back door, and was astonished that Buck was with the pack. I called him over, scolded him harshly, and gave him the only sharp whack he received in his whole life with us. The next morning I was awakened by boisterous barking again. I went to the back door and shouted "Buck!" He emerged from under the back stoop. I petted him and praised him, but he seemed nervous and kept edging in the direction of the uproar. I finally said, "Ok, Buck!" and he ambled over to the pack of barking dogs. He did not join the uproar, however, but sniffed around the others, went over to a bush and peed, and succeeded in leading the pack away! If I had not seen it, I would not have believed such responsible behavior possible.

We stayed in the barracks for three years and then teamed up to look for better housing with three other young couples living in small (but not so primitive) apartments in another part of town.

One of the three young fathers (John McAndrew) was employed by a company that made pre-fabricated Cape Cod cottages. With an architect he knew he worked out a plan to design four variants of a four bedroom ranch house and persuaded his employer to make four prefab models on a trial basis. The architect was willing to work out the plans because he owned some undeveloped land, and hoped to erect a good number of these prefabs. We found four nice lots (about one acre each) in a development that was emerging on an old estate on the west side of Princeton. McAndrew drew on his contacts with builders, roofers, plumbers, and electricians to work out favorable contracts for the construction of four variants of the basic ranch house. The extraordinary end of this good luck is that the company soon changed from making prefabs to making plastic pleasure boats, and we did not have to suffer through witnessing wide spread duplication of our nice houses. We moved in on July 1, 1950, and enjoyed 45 years of pleasant residence.

While we were in the barracks, we took our first family vacation, spending a short holiday in an oceanside resort hotel in Cape May, at the Southern tip of New Jersey. A year or two later on the day we moved into our new house, we put into the house only enough bedding to sleep on; and early the next morning we set out to drive to the Vermont side of Lake Champlain, to a lakeside house that we had located with the help of friends who were natives of Vermont. We arrived at the house to find it a disaster. A few years earlier I had climbed a tree that was covered with a thick vine. The vine turned out to be poison ivy; the inflammation of my arms and legs kept me bedridden for several weeks, and I had acquired extreme susceptibility to poison ivy. Not long before we left for Vermont Buck evidently wallowed in this weed, and I received a severe dose up to the elbow on my left arm. As the infection developed, my arm was grossly swollen and a red streak extended partway to my elbow along a small blood vessel. The doctor said that this was a sign of tetanus and administered a massive injection of penicillin. The infection was healed; the doctor said that were it not for antibiotics, amputation would probably have been necessary. When we arrived at the cottage, we found it surrounded by a sea of poison ivy! We left our luggage in the car, carefully avoided the greenery, made up beds and spent the night.

The next morning we started back to New Jersey, but stopped at a Chamber of Commerce booth in the small town of Vergennes, at a booth labeled "Tourist Information." We asked if there was any sort of resort on the lake that might be suitable for a couple with two young children. They suggested Owl's Head Harbor, about ten miles from Vergennes. We ended on a dirt road that led to a collection of a dozen or more small cottages in the woods along a low cliff over the lake. Each cottage had one or two bedrooms, a living room with a stove or fireplace, and a screened-in porch. There was also a main building with the reception desk, dining room, and kitchen. A two bedroom cottage with a lovely view was available for the three weeks we wanted, at a cost (as I remember) of $36 apiece per week, three meals a day included. Owl's Head proved the nicest vacation spot imaginable. It had a badminton court near the main cottage, and a clay tennis court near the entrance road. "Clay" was the native Vermont clay, scraped and rolled. Steps went down from near the main building to the generally rocky shore of Lake Champlain. Near the bottom of the steps there was a point that formed one boundary of a cove. A small dock was on the point, sand next to the dock formed a small area for wading, and a ladder was a convenience for swimmers. Near this "beach" were anchored several rowboats and on the beach were some canoes. Oars and paddles were available at the main cottage.

A favorite recreation was fishing: still-fishing for perch and trolling for small-mouth black bass. When Sue and I were trolling in shallow water along the shore, the two boys would bring some toys and play at waterside. Buck always stayed near the children. One day, when we in our boat were perhaps 100 feet from the shore, a herd of milk cattle came down to the lake to drink. The availability of lake water was one of the reasons for the prevalence of dairy farming in the area. When Sue saw these large animals approaching her children she insisted we go ashore to rescue them. On shore Buck was dancing in a kind of eager excitement, so I said, "OK, Buck." He hurried around the edge of the herd nipping at heels, and occasionally barking. He rounded up the group and drove them up the hill toward their barn. Two jittery yearlings had separated from the other animals, and run back in the woods. Buck came back, ran behind this pair, and drove them after the others. Back in Princeton, when I described this adventure to a veterinarian I attributed Buck's skill to his collie inheritance. The vet said no; the dog was easily trainable because of his ancestry, but he must have once worked on a farm to be able to herd cattle.

We returned to Owl's Head five or six times and became good friends of the proprietors, Marge and Murray Hoyt. Murray was an occasional journalist, and also wrote some books. One book, about Owl's Head, was entitled: "Does it always rain here, Mr. Hoyt?"

The family spent two summers in West Los Angeles when I was serving as a consultant at RAND, and both times we went across the continent by automobile, sold the car at the end of the summer, and flew back. The long auto trips with two small children were made tolerable by sight-seeing plus planned daytime stops in towns where the AAA listed a playground or a swimming pool. We had a bat and a softball, and a mid afternoon stop for a swim or some baseball broke up the day very well.

When Pete and Rob were still adolescent, the family traveled several times to Europe together. The first trip was occasioned by a meeting of the International Statistical Institute in Stockholm that I had to attend. We went on a Swedish ocean liner from New York to Gothenberg, and by train to Stockholm. After we were out to sea from New York, I went swimming with the boys in the ship's pool, and found the water taken from the North Atlantic extremely cold. It took paternal chauvinism to get me down the ladder into the water. Then I noticed that the Swedish passengers were coming out of the nearby sauna into the pool. When I tried it I found that the very hot sauna felt good after the cold pool, and that the cold was much less uncomfortable if one rushed from the sauna into the pool.

While the meeting in Stockholm was taking place we found opportunities for sight-seeing in the city. The boys and I took a trolley to the harbor, found a sailboat to rent and went for a short excursion in the Baltic. During this trip we developed a system for allowing for the different touristic interests of parents and boys in their early teens. At the beginning of the day in a foreign city we would give each a modest sum in the local currency (enough to pay for lunch and streetcar or subway fares) and say that they must be back at the hotel in time for dinner. They were intimidated enough by being in a strange city with a strange language to stay out of trouble. In Paris they could spend the afternoon as they wanted in the museum of crime, while Sue and I toured the Ile de la Cite.

After the ISI meeting ended in Stockholm, we went by train to Copenhagen. We then rented a car and drove to Paris by way of Rostock,

Amsterdam, Bruges, and Luxembourg. When we left Bruges to pass by Brussels on our way to Luxembourg, Sue found listed in the Michelin Red Guide Book a restaurant in the center of Brussels that specialized in Congolese food. She felt we should seek it out because it might be our only opportunity to sample food from the Congo. I demurred because there was a marginal highway that skirted Brussels and connected to the East-bound route to Luxembourg. There was no need to search out a strange address in the center of a strange city during the noon rush. She regretfully acceded, so we were soon on the broad boulevarde leading East. I saw a bar on our side of the thoroughfare, entered and asked the proprietor to suggest a good place for lunch. He said there was a food market about one block away; it included a small restaurant that catered to the refined tastes of the food stall operators. As I was leaving the bar, he said: "Just a moment. There is a restaurant across the boulevarde that just opened, and I hear it is excellent." We walked across, and had a delicious and exotic meal—in the Congolese restaurant that had just moved from the center of the city!

Another trip *en famille* came two years later before I was to spend a fall semester on leave of absence in Rome. We went to Europe in June, by ship and train to Paris, where we bought a car and drove through the South of France and across the Alps to a small village to the south of the Italian Riviera, where we rented simple quarters for a few days. We were in Monterosso al Mare, one of the Cinque Terre. The Cinque Terre are five villages right on the Mediterranean, where some well–known wine is made. The five little towns were at the time accessible only by foot path and train. The railroad was in a tunnel along the sea, with openings for the stations in the little towns. We parked our car in the last town before this tunnel began and took the train to Monterosso. It was a short walk from our quarters to a spot to swim in the sea, and to excellent local restaurants with good seafood and the famous local wine (for about 20 cents a half-liter carafe).

From Monterosso we went (with overnight stays in Florence and Bologna) to another resort we came to love. It had been found for us by Professor Bernardo Colombo (of the University of Padua), who had spent a year's leave of absence at the OPR. He recommended the Hotel Torri, in Torri del Benaco, on Lake Garda, not far from Verona. The name "Torri del Benaco" is derived from the towers of a medieval castle on the site of the ruins of a Roman Legion fort from classical times; Benacus was the Latin name for Lake Garda.

The part of the town of Torri along the lake appeared to have been unaltered for centuries; indeed the town had been designated a historical treasure, and the small shops were not allowed to make even interior alterations without permission. The hotel was on the lake, across a cove (about a hundred feet wide) from the old castle. It had (I believe) about 15 rooms, of which we rented one with bath on the lakeside for the parents, and one without a private bath for the boys. The hotel's outdoor restaurant was over the shore of the lake. We had access to a bathing establishment maybe 200 yards away. Next to the dock from which we swam was a nice clay tennis court. We transferred to Italy our experience with the sauna and the cold pool on the Swedish liner. We timed our tennis to the hot part of the day, played in bathing clothes, and rushed to dive from the dock when the tennis game was over. When we were thus overheated the cold lake water felt good.

We went back to Lake Garda several times; it reminded us very much of Owl's Head Harbor, including the personal friendliness of the family that owned the hotel. The two lakes are similar, but the cultural environment is very different. For example, we went from the lake to the Roman Arena in Verona one evening to see a performance of "Amletto" in Italian. Hearing "essere o non essere" in a setting nearly 2000 years old was memorable enough, but while we were sitting in the Arena under a clear sky there was a total eclipse of the moon.

From Lake Garda we drove north into Austria, spent one or two days on the Wortersee, and went on to Vienna where I gave a paper at a conference. Then we drove to Rome where Sue and I moved into a pensione, and after a few days sightseeing, the two boys went back to America. One morning before they left, we were waiting for the doors to the Vatican to open, and Pete said, "Mike, I want you to paint the ceiling of my chapel." "OK, Pope, what color?"

The next family trip to Europe was in 1963, when Pete was approaching 21, essentially putting a time lid on voyages by parents and children together. In the fall of 1963 I had a second one–semester leave in Rome, and during the summer I wanted to visit some Eastern European countries to seek data on fertility rates by province for a historical study that had started at the OPR. In this search for historical data, Sue and I visited Vienna, Prague, Warsaw and Budapest, and then returned to Vienna where we were joined by Rob, who had spent four weeks studying French at St. Malo. We drove down through southern Austria and the Dolomite mountains in Northern Italy for a brief stay on Lake Garda, where Pete came up from Perugia to join us. He had studied Italian (plus Etruscan archaeology and the history of Italian art) at the University for Foreigners.

With the family reassembled we went to Trieste (stopping at the

ruins of Aquilea) and on into Yugoslavia, where I visited two internation-
ally known demographic colleagues, Professors Volgenik in Ljudjiana,
and Macura in Belgrade. Volgenik escorted us to an extraordinary secret
hospital in a narrow gully a few miles from Ljudjiana. A small stream with
steep banks appeared to begin with a steep waterfall, but actually there
was a small concealed plateau at the top of the fall, and in this area, during
WWII, the partisans had constructed a small but surprisingly complete
hospital for treating locals wounded by the German or Italian occupiers.
This area was under Axis occupation unlike some mountainous areas to
the South where Tito's troops maintained tenuous control. A remarkable
feature of this hospital is that it remained undiscovered in an area controlled by the occupiers, despite the necessity to carry in the wounded
and bring in supplies. The local population necessarily knew of the hospital all along, but it was never betrayed. One feature of the hospital I shall
not forget is the pictures of Roosevelt and Churchill hung on the wall, left
from wartime.

X

*T*HE DEMOGRAPHIC TRANSITION
AND THE EUROPEAN
FERTILITY PROJECT

In ADDITION to introducing them to analytical demography (including stable population analysis), Notestein as early as 1939–1940, imbued his students and his staff with an interest in the major reductions in fertility and mortality that came to be known as the demographic transition. He was one of the leaders in documenting the reduction in fertility and mortality that had occurred in all of the countries that had by then become industrialized or modernized. He recognized that mortality had generally fallen, first, because of improved availability of food, better habits of personal cleanliness, and, eventually, more effective medicine and public health. Lower mortality and less sickness are always welcome, but lower fertility is not sought until traditional attitudes change. Observing the historic lag between the fall in mortality and in the rate of childbearing, a lag causing a rise in the rate of natural increase, he foresaw a burst of growth in the low income countries, which in 1940 retained high birth and death rates. He foresaw that modern medical technology could be exported from the advanced countries, but that the limitation of births might be adopted only very slowly. He perceived a large potential for accelerated population growth, and thought that it might impede economic development in some of the poorest most densely populated countries. Notestein expressed these ideas in 1939–1941, before large declines in the death rate in many less developed countries had been registered.

The underlying idea of the demographic transition—that modernization, which accompanied industrialization and urbanization in Europe, areas of European settlement, and Japan, is characterized first by a sustained decline in mortality and later by a major reduction in fertility—was based on the records available in a few countries. In particular, the spread of contraception and abortion in these countries was attributed to the social and economic costs of childbearing, which are higher in an urbanized population with industrial occupations, universal education, and female–paid employment, than in a rural population engaged in agriculture, in which young children work on the farm instead of going to school, and women work only in the house and on the farm.

In the early 1960s two graduate students at Princeton engaged in a joint research project in which they examined the change in fertility at the national level in selected European countries. They found parallel declines beginning about 1870 in marital fertility in Hungary and England, despite the contrast between England's pioneering status in industrialization and the spread of education, and the lagging status of Hungary in these developments. Intrigued by these somewhat anomalous findings, I initiated a project to assemble data on the history of fertility in the several hundred provinces of Europe, beginning in each province with the period before the modern decline began, and ending with the most recent data. The data base for this research was the existence of censuses from as early as the late–eighteenth century in a few countries, and by the mid-nineteenth century in many countries, plus the early initiation of the registration of births in most of Europe. The purpose was to document the modern reduction of fertility in geographic detail rather than in a few countries, and to examine the social and economic circumstances in each province when the decline began and as it proceeded. I have sometimes said that if I had foreseen the thousands of hours of work that would be devoted to the study of the history of fertility in Europe, I might not have started the project.

In 1963 a grant from the Population Council made it possible for me to visit Austria, Czechoslovakia, Poland, and Yugoslavia to search for sources of data, and to seek the cooperation of local statisticians and demographers. In subsequent years, we enjoyed the collaboration of Etienne and Francine Van de Walle, Massimo Livi-Bacci, John Knodel, Paul Demeny, Ron Lesthaeghe, Michael Teitelbaum, George Siampos, Vasilios Valaoras, Carl Mosk, Jacqui Forrest, Poul Matthiesson, Barbara Anderson, Susan Cotts Watkins, Erna Harm, Allen Sharlin, and Roy Treadway, to list only those who have published books or journal articles on their research.

In 1979 a summary conference was held near Princeton, to which were invited authors of books and papers that had been part of the project, plus other qualified experts. Those invited to give papers at the conference were asked to look at general questions across countries (such as the relation of infant mortality, urban or rural residence, secularization, and cultural factors to fertility) rather than to restate findings from particular country studies. The proceedings of the conference also include extensive tables, figures, and maps summarizing the level of overall fertility, marital fertility, and the proportion of potentially fertile women married in the provinces of Europe at different dates.

In addition to the proceedings of the summary conference, eight books have been published presenting the analysis of data concerning the decline of fertility in individual European countries. A stream of journal articles still continues. The result has not been a simple version of the transition in fertility, but rather listings and descriptions of exceptions to most of the pre-study generalizations: for example, in a number of provinces, fertility began to fall before mortality; some areas that differed in levels of education and proportions engaged in agriculture but were geographically clustered and shared a language that had parallel declines in fertility. The project showed that there does not appear to be any defined list of social and economic conditions that constitute a threshold for the onset of a sustained decline in fertility.

My own involvement in the project included the trip to eastern Europe in 1963, an intensive study of the decline of fertility in the geographic subdivisions of Russia (in collaboration with Barbara Anderson and Erna Harm), and a mid-project conference on work in progress with authors of several country studies, a conference held in 1969 on the grounds of the magnificent Villa Serbelloni on Lake Como in northern Italy. The Villa had been given some years earlier to the Rockefeller Foundation, and was used for intellectual meetings that enjoy the support of the Foundation. The Villa is at the end of a peninsula where the two south-extending branches of the lake come together, with a view to the north extending to the Alps. The palatial Villa is in the middle of extensive and beautiful gardens, so outstanding that the Michelin tourist guide lists them with three stars, meaning that it is worth a trip from Paris to see them. We were put up in a cluster of buildings on the lake, about a quarter of a mile from the main building. It was a memorable experience: we could swim in the lake before breakfast; our meetings took place in a large room in our buildings, and our meals were brought in from the Villa. The setting was a miraculous treat for the participants, but a logical locale because the participants came from Belgium, Italy, Greece, and Hungary as well as the United States, and it was a more convenient place to assemble than the Eastern United States. The senior secretary of the OPR came to the conference, took notes in short hand, and prepared an eighty-page typescript of our discussion, which has been useful in further research on individual countries.

An amusing episode that occurred during our meeting is an illustration of Demeny's deep Eastern European pessimism. There was a beautiful lawn along the lake beyond our buildings; on some evenings we played *bocce* on the lawn. (An object ball is tossed out on the lawn; opponents try to place their bowling balls closest to the object). When one of two partners is taking the last turn, his teammate goes down near the object ball, and suggests that the bowler aim at the nearest of the opponents' balls, ending up the closest. Paul walked down, looked at the pattern, and said (quite seriously): "It's hopeless!"

XI

$\mathcal{G}$ENERAL OUTLINE
OF MY DEMOGRAPHIC RESEARCH

I SHALL GIVE a lay description of some of my research on population; this autobiography is not the place for a technical summary. To recapitulate, after my general examinations for the PhD in the spring of 1941, and before entering the Navy in early 1942, I was a research assistant at the OPR, engaged in constructing population projections for the countries of Europe from 1940 to 1970. From early 1942 until I returned to the OPR in 1954, I did essentially no demographic research. On my return to the Office, I embarked on several projects, and have continued working on several simultaneously until the time, quite recently, when I began writing this document. In the 1950s I undertook a number of studies involving what might be called analytical or mathematical demography, including problems in "stable population" analysis, the effects of mortality and fertility on age composition, and estimation of undercounts (classified by age, sex, and race) in censuses. The most demanding and important project was a study (with E.M. Hoover) of the relation between population change and economic development in low–income countries. As a result of this research activity, which began as soon as I resumed association with the OPR, in 1959 Notestein proposed that my promotion be reconsidered, and I became both a tenured associate professor, and assistant director of the Office.

In most of my demographic research, I have followed paths that are consistent with the basic interests that guided my education as an undergraduate, graduate student, and radar officer in the Navy. I entered college intending to major in math or physics, and switched to economics, in part, because I thought it more relevant to the social problems of the time. The background I gained in math and physics contributed to my entry into radar work in 1942, and my interest in social problems contributed to my return to economics after the war. I did not find research opportunities that combined my interest in mathematical analysis with my concern for human problems until I returned to population studies.

Mathematical analysis has a natural affinity with the study of population because a population is a denumerable collection of persons, a collection that increases by births and inmigration, and decreases by deaths and out-migration. Each member of a population has an exact numerical age at a specified moment, which is the time that has passed between the individual's birth and the moment in question. Numbers of persons, numbers of births and deaths, numbers of migrants, and the ages of persons and migrants are exact arithmetical values, subject to mathematical manipulation that can be quite subtle and complex, but which is generally rigorous and firmly based in reality. In contrast, mathematical economics deals with such constructs as indifference curves, which cannot be observed and whose numerical counterparts are dubious. The application of Fourier analysis and integral equations to demography is thus intellectually more comfortable than analogous exercises in the application of mathematics to economics.

Demography also encompasses social problems such as the implications of increases in population or of changes in the age composition of a population, and the behavioral sources of changes in fertility and mortality. My own research has moved to and fro among these areas of the field, but has tended to accent analytical aspects of the subject even when dealing with the history of populations, with future prospects, or with social and economic implications. Thus demography has met two of my intellectual drives: the analytical urge that led me to emphasize the study of math and physics when I entered college and the interest in social problems that contributed to my choice of economics as a major when I finished my second year as an undergraduate.

Examples of Research in Analytical Demography: Stable Populations

My work in analytical demography has taken diverse forms. The most abstract form of such analysis that I have undertaken began with Notestein's initiation of his graduate students into the mathematics of stable populations associated with his friend, Alfred J. Lotka. Lotka had proved that a population (not subject to gains or losses from migration) experiencing fixed age schedules of fertility and mortality would come to have a fixed age distribution and fixed overall rates of birth, death, and annual increase. He called such a population "stable" because like a stable physical system, it would return to its fixed rates when disturbed by transitory forces.

In the 1950s I developed new methods for estimating the parameters (such as the growth rate, birth rate, and the death rate) of a stable population, analyzed the process of convergence to stability, and most significantly wrote an article on how the age distribution of a human population is determined, in which I summarized the effects of different

schedules of fertility and mortality on the age composition of the ultimate stable population. I noted that the stable age distribution is determined by the fixed fertility and mortality schedules that have prevailed
for a long period (perhaps a century) and is independent of the schedules
in the more remote past. This process of convergence can be called forget-
ting the past. I offered the conjecture that if a sequence of changing
(rather than constant) fertility and mortality schedules are specified for a
long period, the resultant age distribution is independent of the age distribution at the beginning of the long stipulated sequence of schedules. I
showed the plausibility of this conjecture by projecting from 1860 to 1950
(using the observed schedules of fertility and mortality) a hypothetical
1860 population for Sweden with equal numbers at every age. This projected 1950 population has a proportionate age distribution very little
different from the actual 1950 distribution, suggesting that even when
fertility and mortality are changing, a population "forgets the past." (I illustrate this point for students by asserting that the current age distribution of France is little affected by the Napoleonic wars).

A numerical example does not prove the validity of a proposition; to
my frustration I was unable to find a rigorous proof. As frequently hap-
pens, this extension of the principle of independence of an age distribution from the effects of the remote past to populations with variable histories of fertility and mortality (as well as those with unchanging
schedules) was proved by a brilliant graduate student.

Alvaro Lopez was a Colombian who came to graduate studies at
Princeton by an unusual route. After completing training at the University of Los Andes in Bogota in engineering, he studied advanced mathematics at the Sorbonne. While in Paris he attended a seminar taught by
Louis Henry, the famous French mathematical demographer. He made a
very useful comment on an argument of Henry's and received a note of
acknowledgment from this expert. Later, when Lopez was an attache at
the Colombian embassy in Washington, he met Frank Lorimer at a party
and told him of his encounter with Henry. Lorimer was intrigued and
told Alvaro that he should cultivate this aptitude and apply for a fellowship so that he could take the special graduate training in demography at
Princeton.

In the 1950s Notestein had persuaded Princeton to authorize a special one-year graduate training program in demography, mostly for students from less developed countries. These students followed an individ-
ually tailored course of study, including two intensive one–semester
courses in technical demography, additional courses for particular needs,
such as calculus, advanced statistics, methods of survey research, or de-

velopment economics. Each student was also required to complete an individual research project on a demographic topic under faculty supervision. Successful completion of this visiting student program resulted in the award of a special certificate signed by the president of the University, but did not lead to a formal degree. Many students from a number of less developed countries completed this certificate program, and returned to fruitful careers in their government, in the United Nations, or in academic positions. A high proportion of these special students had their tuition and living expenses paid by fellowships provided by the Population Council in New York. Following Lorimer's suggestion, Lopez applied for admission as a visiting student at Princeton, and for a Population Council fellowship. Both applications were successful.

A few of the more able visiting students supplemented the requirements for the special certificate with some of the regular courses taken by PhD candidates in economics, sociology, or history; they were then accepted as degree candidates. When Lopez arrived, he expressed a strong interest in working toward a PhD. I suggested he might try economics, and he enrolled in first year courses required for admission to the second year of training for the doctorate in economics. He had never taken a course in economics before, but was the top student in every course he took. Princeton does not use accumulated course credits, but does require a candidate for the PhD to pass both oral and written "general" exams in five fields, some of them specified as obligatory. Lopez took his generals at the end of the first semester of his second year, received the highest marks, and was ready to write a dissertation. I suggested to Alvaro that he try to find a proof of my conjecture that even with varying schedules of fertility and mortality, the age composition of a population becomes independent of initial conditions.

I made the suggestion early in February; by the end of May Lopez had found the proof, and incorporated it in a manuscript that also included the use of stable population methods to estimate true rates of childbearing and mortality in recent Colombian history. This dissertation was accepted by the end of his second academic year, and published as a book by the second anniversary of his arrival at the university.

After Lopez had proved that all populations (not merely those subject to unchanging fertility and mortality) are shaped by the recent past, I returned from time to time to some aspect of the mathematics of stable populations (such as the use of Fourier analysis). I wrote a book in 1972 (*The Growth and Structure of Human Populations*) that brought together the various strands of classical mathematical demography I had worked on.

In the past two decades, stimulated in part by ideas cultivated by graduate students, I have helped to think through a generalization to all populations of the role played by the rate of increase in forming the age structure of stable populations, which are characterized by a rate which is the same at all ages. In populations in which fertility and mortality change, the rate of increase varies with age; but there is a general relation between the age schedule of growth rates and the structure of the population that is analogous to relations in a stable population. (Preston and Coale, 1982)

Analytical Research: Detecting and Correcting Bad Data for the U.S.

Another line of demographic analysis that I had engaged in after finishing my general examinations before WWII was correcting population data for errors.(This had been part of my work in 1941 on the future population of Europe). Back at the OPR, I returned to this line by making analytical estimates of the undercount of population (classified by age, sex, and race) in the 1950 census of the United States. Using data on the number of births after 1935 corrected for underregistration, data on mortality and net migration, and various assumptions about similar patterns of undercounts in the three most recent enumerations, I constructed undercount estimates more plausible than those found by the Post Enumeration Survey conducted in 1950. Melvin Zelnik, under my supervision, corrected the native white population listed in the censuses since 1880 by single years of age for age misstatement; in his dissertation he put together annual estimates of white births in the U.S. from 1855 to 1934. Later Zelnik and I collaborated on new single-year estimates of the correct age composition and fertility of the white population after 1880; still later I collaborated with Norfleet Rives on analogous estimates for the black population.

While working with data from the 1950 census, I noted a very odd aberration in the tabulation of marital status by age: the reported number of widows and divorced persons was unbelievably high among young teenagers, and diminished steadily from age 14 to 18. My colleague Fred Stephan who had served as a consultant to the Census came up with an explanation. A very small number of the punch cards on which data were entered had been shifted one column to the right before sorting; the second digit of age became the basis of marital status on these cards. This distortion would be evident only for a very rare category, such as 14 year old widowers. (The shift also created false Indians 10–14 and 20–24). (Coale and Stephan, 1962.)

Correcting Bad Data from Less Developed Countries

An area of analytical demography that I have engaged in intermittently since the 1950s is the search for procedures for manufacturing useable demographic information from the censuses, surveys, and registration figures in the ldc's, in which ages are misreported and omission of persons and events is pervasive.

I was involved with a large project at the OPR in the 1960s, the major part of which was the extraction of the best possible information about population in Africa south of the Sahara. With the exception of countries on the Mediterranean and the Union of South Africa, censuses, surveys, and registered vital statistics for Africa were essentially nonexistent before World War II. Under various auspices, by 1960 data permitting some estimation of fertility and mortality had been gathered for about forty countries with a total population of more than 185 millions. (In 1960 Karol Krotki, who as census commissioner in the Sudan had been involved in the sample census of 1956, completed his PhD thesis at Princeton in which he made estimates of age composition, fertility, and mortality using "quasi-stable" analysis.)

In the fall of 1960 Frank Lorimer accepted a part–time research appointment at the OPR to conduct a reconnoitering survey of the demographic data on tropical Africa. In his survey he made contact with experts who had first-hand experience with the collection and analysis of such data. In 1961–1962 a full-scale project on African population was launched at the Office of Population Research involving Lorimer, William Brass, Paul Demeny, Don Heisel, Anatole Romaniuk, Etienne Van de Walle, and myself. The result of this project was a book published in 1968 in which population totals, age composition, and estimates of fertility and mortality were presented for a large number of geographical areas in sub-Saharan Africa.

Perhaps the most important contribution of this project was the development of methods of estimation employed to tease usable figures from data sources contaminated by incomplete coverage, age misstatement, and other errors. Brass had spent several years at the East Africa Statistical Office, where he had first-hand experience with the inadequacies of African data on population, and had introduced a number of innovations for making bricks with very little straw. Among these was the introduction into censuses and surveys of questions asked of women, about the number of children they had ever borne and the number still surviving. He showed how such data could support robust estimates of fertility and child mortality. In Princeton Brass polished these procedures and collaborated in their application to data from the areas examined in the project. The Coale-Demeny regional model life tables and stable populations were completed while this project was in process, and were extensively applied in the estimates of African population characteristics.

When the study of the population of Africa was finished, Paul Demeny and I undertook the preparation of a manual on Methods of Estimating Basic Demographic Measures from Incomplete Data for the Population Division of the United Nations. The UN Population Commission had recommended the preparation of such a manual, and Demeny and I saw it as consistent with our interest in extending and consolidating the work on Africa.

This Manual (Manual IV) incorporates the methods of estimation and adjustment developed for (and used in) the Africa study. It updates and extends these procedures, and includes inventions specifically developed for the Manual. The emphasis is on presenting techniques in a manner making them accessible to demographers working on data from ldc's. The worked out examples cover populations from nineteenth-century Europe, from Latin America, and from different regions in Asia.

In the past several years I have studied the distortion in old age mortality caused by misstatement of age of persons and age at death among the elderly. With Ellen Kisker I have found that overstatement of age (common among the elderly when knowledge of age is uncertain) leads to understated mortality rates for the very old and is the source of reported lower rates for older black than older white persons, and other examples of mortality "crossovers."

Analytical Research: Creating Demographic Models

Much of my effort in analytical demography has been devoted to the development of "models": typical age patterns (or time patterns) of demographic variables. A schedule of mortality rates is often presented as a life table (an array of death rates by age, accompanied by such implications as the number of persons at each age in a hypothetical cohort subject from birth to these rates.)

A common instance of demographic models is sets of model life tables. Such tables present typical arrays of death rates from the lowest to the highest age intervals at very low to very high overall levels of mortality. Model tables can be formulated because in general when mortality is high or low in some segment of the age span, it is relatively high or low in other segments. In other words, mortality rates at different ages are positively correlated. In 1966 Paul Demeny and I found that among the accurately reported mortality schedules that we could assemble, there were four slightly different clusters of tables with patterns of death rates by age, that within each cluster, went together from high to low overall mortality. One cluster consisted of life tables from Scandinavia, another of mortality schedules from European Mediterranean populations, a third of tables from central and Eastern Europe, and the fourth of mortality tables from accurately recorded mortality in the rest of the world, including western Europe, Northern America, Australia and New Zealand, Japan and Taiwan.

We calculated four sets of model life tables, each embodying the typical age pattern of mortality in one of these clusters at levels of overall mortality from the highest to the lowest on reliable record. (Coale and Demeny, 1966 and 1983). These model tables have been useful in adjusting mortality schedules distorted by erroneous data, for estimating future mortality, and many other purposes.

The models that were particularly enjoyable for me to construct were age patterns of first marriages. The search for a model of the age distribution of entry into first marriage was stimulated by the need to estimate the proportion single at each age in nineteenth-century European populations from census data that listed the total number single and the age distribution of the whole population, but no cross tabulation.

I examined the sequence of the proportion ever married at each age in several European populations in the late-nineteenth and early-twentieth centuries. The curves were distinctly not the same: in some populations marriages began at an earlier age, the proportion married increased more rapidly, and the proportion remaining single was lower than in other populations. Yet when the curves were moved to start at the same point, to have the same average rate of rise and the same final limit of proportion ever married (adjusted in position and scale), it was evident that there was a single standard curve. Don McNeil (an Australian working in the department of statistics at Princeton) and I derived a mathematical expression for the underlying standard schedule of the age distribution of the entry into first marriage, and decomposed it into a sequence of behavioral events: the convolution of the duration of four consecutive stages. The stages were: attaining the age of marriageability in a given culture; finding the ultimate spouse after becoming marriageable; becoming engaged after meeting; and marrying after become engaged. The standard curve adjusted to match the actual distribution in mean and standard deviation fits the actual data very closely, both in very early marrying (mean age at first marriage about 18) and very late marrying (mean age over 25) populations. Etienne Van de Walle guided us to a sample survey of married couples conducted in France in which the age of bride is tabulated by single years, and in which there is also a table giving the duration of acquaintance before marriage. We calculated the expected distribution of this duration as the convolution of the interval between meeting and engagement and engagement and marriage in the standard schedule, which we fitted to the data on age at marriage. In other words, we inferred the distribution of the length of acquaintance before marriage entirely from the table of age at marriage; the fit was very close, except that 10 percent of the respondents are listed as having met more than 6 years before marriage, compared to only 5 percent implied by the mathematical decomposition of the model schedule of first marriages. Couples who stated that they had always known each other were put in the category of having met more than 6 years before marriage. Those who had "always known each other" were (for example) neighbors as children, and did not meet in a way related to their marrying until sometime later. The question should have sought to find out something like when the couple started dating, rather than when they first met. Perhaps only about half of those who "had always known each other" started dating more than 6 years before marriage.

This fit of a mathematically inferred schedule to survey data, although of little or no practical importance, was very gratifying. It was based on a conjecture about the behavioral components of the observed regularity in the age schedule of first marriages. The conjecture led to a correct inference about an empirical distribution of a behavioral component not previously observed.

The correct inference of something not previously inferred or observed is a feature of theoretical physics. A classical example was an inference made by Einstein when he promulgated the general theory of relativity in 1916. At the time he explained exactly the deviation of the orbit of Mercury from the ellipse consistent with Newtonian mechanics (the very powerful gravitation of the sun at Mercury's close proximity causes a precession of its ellipse according to relativistic mechanics). One of the implications of the general theory is that gravitation causes a curvature of space, so that light passing through a strong gravitational field is diverted just as would be a very high velocity massive particle. Hence Einstein predicted that the apparent position of a star whose light beam passed very close to the sun would have a change because of the sun's strong gravity. He made a quantitative estimate of the displacement of a star whose image was to be very close to the sun's disk at the time of the eclipse of the sun that occurred in 1919. Astronomers took their instruments to sea to make observations at a position where the eclipse was total. The apparent position was exactly as Einstein had calculated, and this fact led to unprecedented public attention to a scientific event. (When Einstein was told of this confirmation, he is alleged to have remarked: "If they had not confirmed, their measurements would have been wrong.")

That we correctly approximated the distribution of the interval between meeting and marrying in a sample of French couples from the distribution of their age at first marriage using a mathematical model of entry into marriage, does not make our feat equivalent to Einstein's estimate of the curvature of light passing close to the sun. His discovery is one of the milestones in the history of science; ours is of little importance. Nevertheless, the analogy of predicting something unobserved from a mathematically derived model is quite satisfying. (A further parallel is that at the point where the model does not fit—with fewer couples predicted than reported to have met more than 6 years before marriage—the inclusion of couples who had always known each other may be in effect an error in measurement).

James Trussell and I constructed model schedules of fertility by combining the schedules of proportions married with model schedules of marital fertility, derived from earlier work by Louis Henry. These schedules were derived from Henry's curve of "natural fertility" and a pattern of deviation from natural fertility in a population using control of fertility after attaining the desired number of births. The models fit very closely the accurately recorded schedules with the highest mean age (Sweden 1891–1900), the lowest (Hungary 1970), and with the smallest standard deviation (Japan 1964).

XII

*I*NTERNATIONAL TRAVEL
AS A DEMOGRAPHER

AN ADVANTAGE of my profession that has been much cherished is the opportunity it has provided for ranging over the world. Some years ago I started noting the dates of each foreign trip I took, listing the places visited, and the reason for the trip. These entries are kept in a folder in a drawer near my desk. Because of this custom I know that I have been in seventy-seven countries, and have made ninety-one visits to Europe. This extensive perambulation has been occasioned by research, consultation, lectures, and other professional missions. Very few trips were for personal tourism: I have paid for transportation on but twelve of the ninety-one visits to Europe. The major advantage of professional instead of touristic travel is not reduced cost but the intimate experiences one has with colleagues and institutions.

My first trip ever outside of North America was to gather information on the Indian population and the Indian economy for the research project that Ed Hoover and I began in 1954. I briefly described our experiences in India; they were part of a trip around the world.

Our visit to India in the fall of 1955 was before the days of travel by jet plane. Having some unused vacation time, Sue and I thought of allocating about a week extra for stopovers en route to New Delhi. My brother Jim, who had lived in Germany for a few years after the war, advised us to spend several days in one country rather than trying to visit London, Paris, Geneva, Rome, etc. He also recommended Italy for the several day visit. So we flew on a Pan Am Clipper to Paris (with a refueling stop at Shannon), and twenty-four hours later flew to Rome, where we saw the Forum and the Colosseum before taking a super express train to Florence. This train had a curved front across the first car, with a picture window that gave a spectacular view up the track. (The engineer was seated on an upper level). As the train pulled out of Rome we moved to this special club car to find all of the front seats occupied. An Italian gentleman, recognizing that we were foreigners, came back and asked Sue if she would not like a seat with the view. Somewhat hesitantly she assented; he took her up and told his wife to give up her seat! An early introduction to Italian male chauvinism!

In Florence we stayed at the Pensione Tornabuoni, which belonged to a Contessa who was so pleased with our enthusiasm for Florence that she treated us very well indeed, recommending restaurants and sights not to miss. I remember vividly walking along a back street parallel to the Arno, turning a corner and having a full view of the Piazza della Signoria with its magnificent Renaissance buildings and famous statuary.

On this visit I had a memorable introduction to the contrast between the attitudes of the French and the Italians to foreign attempts to speak their language. When we realized in Florence that we had no hotel reservation for our scheduled overnight layover in Athens, I went to an American Express office near the river. It was after 6:30, and a sign said that the office would reopen at 7:00. I stepped into a neighboring bar, and with the help of a pocket dictionary tried to explain that I wanted a Martini made with gin. When I had found the right words, the bartender asked how long I had studied Italian. I used the dictionary again and answered three days. Then I looked up the word for "build," found the infinitive "costruire" and said "non costruire Roma"; he laughed, and added "en un giorno!" In Paris, when I ask for a room in decent French, the clerk answers scornfully in English.

When we arrived at the Athens airport the evening after leaving Rome, we took a taxi to the hotel American Express had found for us; it was several miles to the north of the city, but very pleasant, especially after we found out that the proprietor knew John Rockefeller, whom we had met because of his interest in population. Our flight to Cairo was to depart well after dinner on the next day. On the next day the hotel host generously took us into the city in his own car; we left our luggage at the airline office and visited the Agora, the sights on the Acropolis, and the National Museum. After dinner we returned to the airline office to connect with our evening departure to Egypt. We were told that the flight had been delayed until midnight, so we walked up a stairway to the gate in the wall around the Acropolis, and found it closed. We walked to the top of a cliff near the gate, looked down, and saw a Greek play, complete with chorus, taking place in an open-air Roman theater! When we returned to the airline we were told the flight would leave the next morning, and that we were being taken to an out-of-town hotel for the night. It turned out to be the same hotel we had stayed in, and Sue and I were treated royally.

In Cairo we squeezed in a hurried visit to the pyramids and the Sphinx before flying on toward India. British Air flew us to the Karachi airport where after several hours we were to fly Air India to New Delhi. The British stewardess advised us not to try to visit Karachi, and offered to arrange a room in Speedbird House, a rest facility for British Air personnel. When we had been introduced to the desk clerk, he called a bell-boy and said "Take Sahib and Memsahib to their room." Pretty exotic for a first trip out of America!

In India we supplemented our visits to community development projects, health facilities, local authorities, etc., with one weekend of pure tourism. The Coales and Hoovers hired a car with driver, went to Agra and saw both the Taj Mahal and Fatepur Sikri. Sue and I continued around the world after the mission in India, stopping in Rangoon, Bankok, Hong Kong, Tokyo, and Honolulu. On my first trip outside the United States, we saw Notre Dame Cathedral, the Colosseum, the Uffizi, the Acropolis, the pyramids, the Taj Mahal, the canals in Bankok, a floating restaurant in Hong Kong, the imperial palace in Tokyo, and Diamond Head in Hawaii. I agree with my brother that it was wiser to spend a week in Italy than to rush through many European capitals, but the fame of the world's best known sights is justified, and I remember them with awe.

No other trip in connection with a research project can match this first one, but we have become at least more than a little familiar with many countries that we would not have visited on pure pleasure travel. Our more than thirty visits to Italy, including three stays of at least a semester, more than fifteen visits to Paris, and twenty to London, make us feel more or less at home in three foreign countries. Even the Italian, French, and London English languages do not seem discordant. We have also been acculturated to some degree in China, Mexico, Pakistan, Thailand, Australia, Turkey, Kenya, the Phillipines, Greece, Brazil, and Egypt. Join demography and see the world!

XIII

$\mathcal{P}$ROFESSIONAL ACTIVITIES IN DEMOGRAPHY OUTSIDE THE UNIVERSITY

DURING THE PAST SEVERAL DECADES I have been called upon to undertake a number of professional missions, which have provided me with rewarding friendships, professionally enriching knowledge, and, often, enjoyable and enlightening travel. The first such mission that I recall was serving as the United States representative to the Population Commission of the United Nations.

The United Nations Population Commission

When Notestein, on part–time leave from the OPR, served as the Founding Director of the Population Division of the United Nations, he also helped establish another UN body, the Population Commission, whose function was more or less legislative in population matters. Selected member nations were invited to appoint a representative on the Commission, which met for two weeks every other year, to recommend the agenda of UN population activities, primarily in the Population Division and the Statistics Division. When the Commission was established, Notestein had envisaged as its members a group of professional demographers who would review the recent demographic activities of the UN, and recommend what should be done in the future.

In 1961 I was invited to accept appointment as the US Representative to the Commission. It was a presidential appointment entailing confirmation by the Senate, a process which implied for the appointee only that he had to fill out forms listing all his places of former residence and former positions as part of an FBI security check. The appointment was by President Kennedy; the recommendation came from a state department official with some responsibility for personnel, a former Princeton student, Harlan Cleveland, who had lived in a room near my brother's when an undergraduate. When I went to Washington to be briefed on my responsibilities, I reminded the briefing officer of Notestein's intention that the Commission be a technical body, and said that I conceived my role as giving expert advice rather than serving as a representative of US political positions. I was reassured that the State Department wanted me to present my own ideas and use my own technical judgment. There might arise a question on which the US had a firm political position (such as whether China should be invited to membership on the Commission) and I might be instructed what to say. I was told that under these circumstances I should ask for the floor and state: "I have been instructed to say . . . ," thus clearly distinguishing a political statement from my professional advice. This situation never arose while I served on the Commission.

During my six years on the Commission the meetings became increasingly tedious. The original concept of a Commission of demographic experts evolved toward a Commission of persons appointed to represent political positions in their countries. In some instances the resident representative of the country at the UN headquarters in New York served as the country's Commission member. Political positions became ever more prominent in the discussions. For example, the representatives of Russia, the Ukraine, or Poland would insist that the word "fertility" should not appear in the Commission documents, because it is a Malthusian term inconsistent with Marxist thought.

There were genuinely top flight demographers present, such as Louis Henry and Jean Bourgeois-Pichat from France, the Registrar General of the UK (Bernard Benjamin, and later John Borham), W.D. Borrie of Australia, and others, but in the discussion and in the composition of the reports, much irrelevant material had to be sidetracked. The Commission elected a rapporteur who presented his draft of the report as the meeting approached its end. Every sentence was likely to be challenged, and progress through the report was very slow. On the last day, when the delegates were eager to have some time for shopping before leaving New York, adoption of the report speeded up, and at the end of the last afternoon the full text was accepted. Then the delegates praised the chairman, the rapporteur, the translators, and the pages, and the meeting was over. Before I was appointed to the Commission, the OPR had received the Commission reports every two years, but I had never read them. When one of the Commission meetings ended, I went to the center of the room to say goodbye to my friends, and encountered Bourgeois-Pichat. "B.P.," I said, "This may be the only report with more authors than readers!" "No, no," he replied, "the *same number* of authors and readers!"

I remember two amusing experiences with my good friend John Borham, who was the representative from the UK. Each year, the two-week meetings in New York were interrupted by a break from Friday to Monday; I went home to Princeton for this weekend. I invited John to join me as our guest. After we had spent Friday evening, Saturday, and

Sunday at our house, I warned him that to get to the Monday meeting on time, we would need to get up at six o'clock on Monday morning. "You did not tell me that!," he remarked. The second experience was some years later at a meeting on demography at Ditchley Park, near Oxford. John was chairman of a session, and after he declared the session at an end, I made an additional remark. I apologized for continuing to talk after he had called adjournment. He said: "I knew I could depend on you!"

In 1967 the Commission met at the UN headquarters in Geneva, a locale that made possible a pleasant visit to Switzerland. The US arrangement for the meetings of the Commission included provision for an advisor to the Representative, usually an expert from the Census Bureau who sat at my shoulder during the meetings. In Geneva a citizen advisor was appointed in addition to the expert. When I arrived in Switzerland I went to our embassy to touch base, and found that President Johnson had appointed as the citizen advisor, a friend of the President from Texas: Emma Long, the mayor of Austin. The only message to the embassy from the White House about the meeting of the Commission was to take good care of Emma. I went to the meeting room at UN headquarters with some anxiety about the presence of this Texan lady during the meetings. My concern was mistaken. The opening item of business was the choice of the rapporteur. A potentially disastrous instance of the politicization of the commission was the nomination of a non-demographic representative from an African country, a man who lacked any evidence of skill in writing. I began to evolve a strategy for getting support for a more suitable choice, when Emma Long said, "This is important, isn't it?" I concurred, and she then asked if she could do some lobbying in the corridors during the recess. She did, and a qualified rapporteur was chosen.

At the end of the meetings I had developed respect and fondness for Emma Long. I had learned that she was an unusual Texas mayor, having desegregated the public athletic facilities, for example. In Geneva she worked hard on mastering population issues, and continued to make useful suggestions about tactics.

Advisory Missions to African Countries

In 1965 the government of Kenya asked the Population Council to send a team of experts to Kenya to study its population problems, and to make recommendations about determining and attaining an ideal rate of growth. The Council agreed to send a mission, and I was asked to be a member, along with Richmond Anderson, director of technical assistance at the Council; Lyle Saunders of the population program at the Ford

Foundation, and Howard Taylor, chairman of Obstetrics and Gynecology at Columbia.

The mission spent three weeks in Kenya, meeting some twenty-five government officials in the Capital, and visiting hospitals, clinics, and schools at the coast, and in the west, north, and south of the country. (We also spent a half day driving around the game park not far from Nairobi, where we saw many animals, including hippopatomi and a pride of lions lunching on a slain zebra).

While we toured the country in a car provided by the Ford Foundation, guided by a junior official from the Ministry of Economic Planning, we saw the health facilities and schools in the rural areas of the different regions. While in a rural area north of Nairobi we were invited to be present at a meeting of a family planning worker and a group of her clients. The family planning worker made her talk to the local women, and then offered to translate any questions we wanted to ask. When my colleagues asked about contraceptive practice, there was much giggling. Our interlocutor explained that such subjects were not discussed with strangers, and that the women were embarrassed. I then asked if the women were aware that the mortality rates among their children were lower than the rates when they were children. More giggles. I asked if child mortality were a ticklish subject. She said no, but everyone knows that mortality is much lower than earlier, so why did I ask them about their knowledge. Finally we inquired if any of the women wished to ask us questions. One of the ladies asked if family limitation were practiced in the United States, and we said yes, for many decades. Then why had we not come to Kenya much earlier?

During our many tours on the roads of Kenya, I had a prolonged argument with Howard Taylor about the poor record of the medical profession in attaining low mortality rates in the United States. Infant mortality was lower in Hong Kong and Singapore than in the U.S.; when the Salk vaccine became available, the AMA in New Jersey voted to ban from hospital facilities doctors who offered to administer the vaccine free of charge. (Our argument was friendly and low key, but, off and on, it persisted for several days). When we were in the west of Kenya, in Kisumu, we were invited to tea in the home of the president of the local family planning association. I was conversing with some of the local members when I heard the host ask Dr. Taylor whether the television show "Dr. Kildare" was a valid representation of medicine in America. Taylor replied "Let's ask Professor Coale that question."

The mission submitted a report to the government of Kenya, summarizing the importance of a population program in the country and making many suggestions about its design and implementation. The report was published in 1967 by the ministry of economic planning and development. It was many years before effective family planning activities on a national scale began; neither the political climate nor individual attitudes were ready, although they have finally become so.

I have had several other pleasant visits to Kenya—to attend an African population conference, to serve as an outside examiner at Nairobi University, and to attend a meeting of the steering committee of the World Fertility Survey, a meeting held in Kenya at a date to coincide with the WFS Kenyan survey.

In 1967 the government of Morocco asked the Population Council to send a mission of experts to give advice on Morocco's population problems and possible policies. The Council was forced to modify its first plan, which was to assemble a group not only of Americans, but also of persons with recent experience in the Near East. The outbreak of the Six Day War unsettled the atmosphere in Arabic countries, even those as distant from the war as Morocco, but the Council learned that the sponsors of the mission felt it crucial not to cancel the trip. The visiting group was reduced to Parker Mauldin of the Council and myself. We concentrated on obtaining visas in time to meet our scheduled departure. The plan to have Sue go with us was abandoned.

We enjoyed the visit to a beautiful and fascinating country very much, talked to many government and local people, wrote a careful report, but had no dramatic effect on the initiation of active population policy in Morocco.

As part of our mission, Parker and I made a visit to Marrakech in the foothills of the Atlas mountains. When we arrived we found it was Mohammed's birthday, and the offices we were to visit were closed. We went for a walk around the colorful city, and on a street lined with shops came to a store selling oriental rugs, which was open despite the holiday. Parker said that it would be fun to bargain for a rug, although neither of us really wanted to buy one. I reluctantly went along. Parker found a beautiful modest sized rug, featuring a diamond shaped pattern of tan stripes on a white background. No dye had been used; both the background and the stripes were natural wool. The proprietor quoted a price of $200; Parker offered $100, including shipping. The owner rejected this as ridiculous, and then offered successively lower figures until he finally accepted the offer. If Parker had really intended to buy a rug, I doubt if he could have held out.

While we were in Morocco we learned that the tension caused by the Six Day War was over, and travel to Morocco was no longer restricted.

When Sue had learned that she could not accompany me to Morocco, she had arranged a European trip with our daughter-in-law. I looked at their itinerary, reached Sue by phone at her hotel in Rome, and arranged to meet her in Casablanca when our mission was over. When she arrived we rented a car and drove to Agadir, near which there was a Club Mediterrane. We had a wonderful short holiday at this seaside resort, which had a nice beach, good recreational facilities, and exceptional food. One morning we drove to a nearby souk, found a rug merchant and bought two 9 by 12 carpets with the same design as Parker's bargain, except that the stripes were made of natural black, rather than tan, wool. Profiting from experience, we got a good price, including shipment. I asked how the rugs should be cleaned, and the proprietor said that he washed them in the sea.

In 1966 I went to Nigeria to a conference on Nigerian population statistics. Because of political contention between inhabitants of different regions, the results of the 1960 census were useless. I had two quite different adventures on this trip. I flew to London on my way, to make connections with a flight from London to Lagos. The Pan Am flight arrived in London after the departure to Lagos. I explained that my transatlantic flight was useless unless I went on to Nigeria. The airline ticketed me to Zurich and then non stop to Lagos on Lufthansa first class (the only space available). The second adventure was caused by the civil unrest in Nigeria. Our meeting was in Ibadan, and the Nigerian hosts provided a private car from the airport in Lagos to Ibadan. There was a human cordon across the highway en route formed by a group of dissidents, a frightening sight for a foreign visitor. The driver pulled off the road just beyond the human blockade, down shifted and zoomed off safely.

In 1971 I was asked to travel to Zaire to consult with officials about establishing relations between the demographers representing the US National Research Council and population experts in Zaire.

No effective results were accomplished in part because the country was in a state of political chaos. I remember being warned to avoid soldiers when walking outside the hotel because army personnel were robbing tourists.

Advisory Missions to Latin America

In 1964 the UN-supported center for demographic training and research in Latin America (CELADE) was putting a strain on the funds for population work at the United Nations, which were supplying the financial support for the Center. A proposal was made to transfer the financial support to the general UN fund for social and economic development. I was asked to visit the Center in Santiago, Chile, to recommend whether the support was warranted. I went to New York to talk to the appropriate authority at the UN, and explained that I knew in advance that I would recommend support, because I was familiar with the publications that had come out of CELADE, and from my acquaintance with some of the graduates, knew that the training must be excellent. Moreover, the director, a Panamanian named Carmen Miro, was a skilled demographer of unusual integrity and force of character. Holding these strong opinions, perhaps I was not the right person to make an evaluation. I was told that there was no doubt at the UN that CELADE deserved support, but Carmen might need help in drafting the request for funds.

I decided to accept the assignment. The UN invited me to send them our passports, so that they could get visas for Sue and me. The day before our departure I went to the UN for last minute advice. The passports had not been taken to the consulates for visas; I found out from the airline that we could debark at Lima (our first stop) without visas; we visited Lima, Buenos Aires, and Rio de Janeiro similarly, short of documents. Routine procedure is not one of the strengths of the United Nations.

At CELADE my favorable impression of Carmen Miro was strengthened. I knew, from having visited the UN's Asian population center in Bombay, that one of the difficulties in operating a regional center is that the governments in the area insist on choosing the trainees, and select poorly qualified persons. I asked Carmen if this was a problem in Latin America. She said yes, but she had solved it. Indeed government officials nominate unqualified friends and relatives; but CELADE had started an entrance examination; whoever did not pass was sent home.

While in Santiago I talked with the members of CELADE's staff. I had never studied Spanish, but had become a little accustomed to hearing it on earlier trips to Mexico. I had, however, become fluent in Italian. At CELADE I had a one hour conversation with one of the professors in which, speaking slowly, he used Spanish, and I used Italian. There were some words in which the resemblance was not close enough for comprehension, for example: "los indios" and "gli indiani."

In 1968 I was asked to survey the population program of the Ford Foundation in Latin America, and make whatever suggestions I thought suitable. I recall in particular my experience with the Ford population program in Brazil. In Brazil the Foundation had been trying to promote more widespread and more effective birth control. It supported the work of the Brazilian private family planning organizations, and subsidized the manufacture of contraceptives within the country. Strong opposition was expressed to the Ford population program from the left wing (generally Marxist), from the Church, and from the government, dominated by the military. The Ford activities were denounced as part of Yankee imperialism: as an effort to reduce the numbers in the proletariat and the peasantry in Brazil. The military favored a high birth rate to provide manpower to protect the large Brazilian territory from powerful neighbors. When I wrote my report to Ford, I suggested that the Foundation should tone down its direct efforts to reduce fertility in Brazil because of the negative effects of these efforts on public opinion. I suggested further that it should start a program that would have a delayed, but, I thought, a fairly certain payoff. I knew that at the time there were a number of Brazilian university graduates in economics or other social science who went abroad for graduate study, and that they did unusually well at outstanding universities in the US and Europe. I suggested a Ford policy of subsidizing the postgraduate study of some of the best of these students if they would include the graduate study of demography in their curriculum while abroad. Excellent population training was available at many of the universities where these Brazilians went. In the ensuing years a number of Ford fellows were appointed and indeed included advanced demography in their graduate studies at foreign universities.

The Ford Foundation representative in Brazil conjectured that the acceptance by the government during the 1970s of family planning was partly the result of the demographic training received by the elite students who had postgraduate work at foreign universities. Before the Ford fellowships, the Brazilians trained abroad returned to important positions in Brazil: in government agencies or universities. When the fellowships had been in effect for a few years, these young experts had learned basic demographics, including the concept of population momentum. Momentum implies that a population with a high rate of increase because of high fertility and low mortality continues to increase rapidly even after childbearing has fallen to a level where couples are having children at a rate that just replaces the parents. The reason for continued rapid growth is that when fertility has fallen to this low level, the rapid growth of the young population that is the residue of past high fertility means a continued increase in the number of parents and in the number of births. If the Brazilian population of the early 1960s had immediately adopted fertility at the replacement level, the population would increase by about 50 percent by the end of the century; if fertility smoothly declined to replacement by 2,000, the population would about double.

According to the Foundation representative in Brazil, when government officials heard this information from young expert Brazilian advisors rather than from US spokesmen, and as rising pressure for family planning emerged, they responded, "An increase of 50 to 100 percent sounds sufficient, why not let family planning proceed."

Whether or not this conjecture is valid, there is no doubt that demography in Brazil has flourished since the fellowships were begun. In 1969 there were ten Brazilian members of the IUSSP, the international organization of scientific demographers; in 1994 there were thirty-nine Brazilian members. In those twenty-five years the number of Brazilian members was multiplied by more than four; the total membership of the IUSSP about doubled.

Consultant to Population Institute, Haceteppe University, Ankara

In 1967 the Ford Foundation decided to support the establishment of a population research and training center at Haceteppe University in Ankara, Turkey. I was asked to go to Ankara to advise the director on the staffing and program of the center. I went to Ankara, talked to the director and other officials, and visited the small community in which some demographic data collecting had been begun. I then formulated a long agenda, including courses to be taught, qualifications the students should have, and the design and staffing of a continuing program of data collection and analysis in the nearby community. I had my suggestions typed up in the local Ford office, and gave the typescript to the director in the two–hour car trip to the airport. He read it carefully and handed it back saying, "We'll do it."

Chairman of the Academy of Sciences Committee on Population

In 1976, I started a fall–term leave of absence by going to the International Institute of Applied Statistical Analysis, outside Vienna. I then had a brief stay in Florence, before proceeding to the East-West Institute of population studies in Honolulu. While in Hawaii, I received a phone call asking me to serve as chairman of a new committee of the National Academy, a committee on population. The Academy had been asked to form such a committee by the Agency for International Development (AID) of the State Department.

The request from AID to establish an NAS committee on population arose because the very vigorous AID program in support of family planning under the active administration of "Ray" Ravenholt had caused some tension. Ravenholt had sought to create a statistical group that would issue estimates showing that AID's support of family planning programs in certain less developed countries had helped reduce fertility. He had allegedly put pressure on a group in the Census Bureau that, with AID support, made estimates of fertility trends in LDCs, pressure to produce estimates favorable to the record of the AID population program. The top administrators of AID, fearing repercussions from these allegations, asked the Academy to form a committee to make the best possible estimates of current fertility and mortality in less developed countries.

When I went to Washington to discuss the membership, the staff, and the agenda of the new committee, I found that AID had designated Ravenholt and his assistant to represent the agency at these discussions. Ray said to me that he wanted the committee to prepare fresh estimates each year of fertility and mortality in all the LDC's, especially those in which AID had, or was considering, a program of assistance. I replied that if he wanted such estimates, he could look them up in the United Nations Statistical Yearbook. My ideas for the committee were that it would include leading experts on the demography of the third world, on methods of evaluating the quality of population information in LDC's, and on extracting usable information from inaccurate data.

The committee would select particular countries to be studied intensively, on the basis of their population size, and the possibility of arriving at valid conclusions about important trends. The method of operation would be to appoint a panel of experts on each country consisting of at least one member of the committee, other suitable American or European specialists, and a number of appropriate officials and scholars from the country in question. If, instead, the function of the committee was to assemble annual figures on a long list of different countries, I did not want to serve on it.

David Goslin, the director of the Commission on Behavioral and Social Sciences of the National Research Council (the operating arm of the Academy of Sciences) accepted my ideas for the Committee. He said that my response to Ravenholt showed that I knew how to play hardball. We chose eleven leading demographers and statisticians to be members of the committee (six were then or later became members of the Academy) and went to work. By 1985 the committee had published twenty-eight reports, including fourteen on individual country estimates, and many methodological treatises. We hired a professional staff, with Robert Lapham as study director, and Ken Hill, Jane Durch, and Hania Zlotnik as expert collaborators and coordinators of the panels.

As the steps for establishing the committee proceeded, I returned to the East-West Population Institute in Honolulu, where I was spending the last part of a fall–term leave of absence. Lee Jay Cho, director of the Insti-

tute and a member of the NAS committee, and I began to put together for
the Republic of Korea corrected single-year age distributions for the census years of 1955, 1960, 1966, 1970, and 1975, plus estimates of fertility
and mortality from 1955 to 1975. Noreen Goldman who had come to the
OPR (from Harvard) as a research assistant at the end of 1977 flew to Hawaii for a month early in 1978 to work with Lee Jay, members of the staff
at the East-West center, and myself on the Korean study. Noreen and I returned to Princeton and continued our labors in collaboration (by telephone and mail) with our Honolulu colleagues. Report No. 1 of the committee by Noreen, Lee Jay, and me was published in 1980.

Reports 2 and 3 were also published in 1980, on Thailand and Honduras, respectively. The Thai Report was the work of a panel consisting of
three Thai and three American population specialists, as well as Ken Hill,
the Senior Research Associate of the committee. Hill was the author of the
report on Honduras. The Thai report was very typical of how individual
countries were handled by the committee: by recruiting a panel of experts
both from the country in question and from the US and Europe, and bas-
ing a report (drafted with the help of the committee staff) on the work of
the panel. By 1982, 168 population specialists, 94 from less developed
countries, had served as members of panels or working groups.

My own most memorable involvement in country studies undertaken by the committee was work incorporated in the reports on Egypt
and China (Reports Nos. 9 and 27). On the basis of the Committee's cri-
teria for selecting countries, Egypt was a strong candidate to be the subject of a report. Establishment of a panel on Egypt was delayed a bit because data from a crucial source (the census of 1976) were not yet
available, and the responsible statistical body in Egypt, the Central
Agency for Public Mobilization and Statistics or CAPMAS, had a reputation for reluctance to release data, especially to non-Egyptians. Its director, General Gamal Askar, was allegedly a prickly person who might not
be cooperative with the committee. I had the idea, in forming a panel on
Egypt, to include, as usual, several Egyptian authorities, and to designate
General Askar and myself as cochairs of the panel. I wrote to Askar explaining how the committee worked, the importance we gave to Egypt,
the necessity to have several Egyptians on the panel, and the value of having both the chairman of the NAS Committee and the head of CAPMAS
involved in guiding the work. Askar agreed, and assumed responsibility
for assembling and initially processing the data, while I assumed primary
responsibility for supervising and carrying out the analysis. There were
three meetings of the panel in Cairo. Jane Durch (of the committee staff)
and I did much of the analysis and the composition of the report. A grat-

ifying feature of the cooperation of CAPMAS was that all of the crucial tabulations of the 1976 census were made available to the panel, some before they were published in Egypt. We also enjoyed the full cooperation of the CAPMAS staff, in addition to the invaluable help of the six Egyptian members of the panel. The report includes estimates of corrected age and sex distributions every five years from 1927 until 1977 (and at the census dates in 1960 and 1976) plus estimates of annual birth rates, death rates, total fertility, infant mortality, and life expectancy.

The report on China, which I wrote, has only an indirect connection with the regular work of the NAS Committee. I had first become involved with the population of China in the mid 1970s when Irene Taeuber, shortly before her death in 1974, became intrigued with data Notestein had retained in unpublished form: tabulations from a large demographic survey of rural China conducted in 1929–1931 by the Nanking Agricultural College under the direction of Lossing Buck. The demographic information was collected in connection with a survey of land usage in China. When the three volumes on land usage were published in 1937, Notestein and a Chinese colleague contributed some 40 pages on population, and Frank also published a paper on the survey data in 1938. The fertility and mortality rates found in the survey seemed low to many; in fact Notestein rejected the data from communities in which birth or death rates were below the 25th percentile, because some were so low as to be clearly incredible, a flaw not surprising, given the circumstances of the survey. Thus most scholars were unwilling to accept the fertility and mortality rates derived from the survey as representative of rural China. Irene Taeuber, who had become engrossed with the population of China in the last years of her life, knew of the tabulations which Notestein had kept from the 1929–1931 survey, tabulations that would be suitable for analysis by procedures developed since Frank had worked on the Buck survey material. The procedures were those that had been used in studying the demography of Tropical Africa, and those later employed by the panels of the NAS committee. By combining different sorts of imperfect data, valid age schedules of fertility and mortality could be constructed for the Chinese rural population around 1930.

Several years after this historical analysis (in 1976), I became involved with Chinese population again. I was asked in 1980 to help strengthen technical demography in China by giving a series of lectures at People's University in Beijing, to an audience of potential university and government demographers. While on this mission (described later) I had a meeting with Chen Mu Hua, a vice premier who had nominal responsibility for population policy in China. I said to her that demography in

China could not progress very far when fundamental data such as the results of the censuses taken in 1953 and 1964 had not been published, meaning that Chinese demographers could hardly do serious empirical work. Another suggestion I made to Chen Mu Hua was that some of the very able young men finishing their studies at Chinese universities, those who had skills in foreign languages, and some training in a social science plus mathematics and statistics, should be sent abroad for graduate training in demography. As I was leaving the audience room, I caught up to Sue who said, "How about the able young women finishing their studies?" I turned back to the Vice Premier and repeated through the translator what Sue had said. She smiled and made a thumbs-up gesture.

In 1982–1983, while spending a year on leave from Princeton at the Institute for Advanced Studies in the Behavioral Studies at Palo Alto, I became involved in assisting Professor Arthur Wolf of Stanford University to analyze the results of interviews he had conducted in 1980-1981 with elderly women in seven communities in China. This involvement in Chinese demography, plus the availability of the results of the three Chinese censuses and the large sample survey on fertility, led me to start an analysis of population trends in China since 1952. When I returned to Princeton I completed this work, finding excellent consistency between data from the censuses and the survey. I calculated schedules of fertility, mortality, and first marriages over a thirty year time span. Methods that had been used in the committee work on other countries were employed (and sometimes extended). The results were written up in a manuscript of about 90 pages. I wondered where to find a publisher. I called Bob Lapham who was approaching completion of his duties as study director of the NAS committee, and asked his advice about publication. He said "Why not issue it as a report of the Committee?" The committee had strongly desired a panel on China, but felt that the data were insufficient; instead of trying to form a panel at such a late date, it could just name the chairman as in effect a one man panel on China.

After the report on China was issued, the Academy asked me to come to Washington for a press conference. It turned out that most of the reporters were interested in a small point: the 1982 fertility survey had noted that the ratio of male births to female births reported for 1981 was higher at higher order than at lower–order births. I stated that this rise in sex ratio with order of birth could not be true. It indicated that some of the higher–order female births had been omitted from the birth histories. I mentioned that because the one-child policy had been introduced recently, higher–order births had become taboo; respondents might fail to report a recent third birth, and omit such a birth more often if it were a female, because of the traditional pride in bearing a son. I also mentioned rumors of the reappearance of female infanticide, and said that it might be a factor. It was the possibility of infanticide that the press wanted to hear about. I repeated that the higher sex ratio at higher orders was evidence that some higher–order female births had been omitted, but whether omission occurred because the birth was opposed by the authorities or because of female infanticide could not be judged from available information. I was then asked if infanticide were the reason, how many girl babies would need to have died. I repeated that I did not believe it to be the reason, then reluctantly did a rough calculation in my head and came up with a large number, adding that it was highly implausible. The *Washington Post* and other papers represented at the press conference carried a low-key story on the China Report, but a tabloid quoted me as saying that many thousands of female babies had been killed.

A little later, *The Economist*, in an article on the population of China, quoted me as saying that 250,000 female babies had been killed after the one-child policy had been introduced (evidently having picked up the item from the account in the tabloid). I wrote a letter explaining that I had not made such a statement and remarking that I found their misquote an instance of irresponsible journalism. I did not receive a response in the mail, and expressed my frustration to my older son's wife who is a gifted administrator. She suggested that I call the New York office of *The Economist*, and to get the attention of a person of authority, say that I wanted to speak with someone authorized to discuss litigation.

I followed her advice, and immediately was put through to a senior person who asked if I had not seen my letter. I explained that I did not subscribe to the journal. He said that the letter had been published, and added that because of a shortage of space, letters were edited, not for content but for length. I found a copy of the issue that contained my letter, and found it complete except for the statement that I found *The Economist* guilty of irresponsible journalism!

Three years later an article on world population in *The Economist* again included a statement attributed to me that 250,000 girl babies had been killed in China. My letter this time was quite irate. I said that their journalism was inept as well as irresponsible since they themselves had published my earlier disavowal of this statement. Later at the demographic conference at Ditchley Park near Oxford mentioned earlier the chairman announced that a staff writer from *The Economist* was keeping notes and would prepare a summary of our discussion. At a coffee break I asked the journalist if he knew about the difficulty I had had with his employer. "I'll say," he replied, "I wrote the piece." He then told me the reassuring news that *The Economist* had revised its procedures, and now routinely checked its correspondence files while preparing its text for publication.

Involvement in the World Fertility Survey

The World Fertility Survey, planned beginning in 1972, partially in connection with the anticipated World Population Year of 1974, was led by the International Statistical Institute (ISI), in collaboration with the IUSSP, and the Statistical Office and the Population Division of the United Nations. It began operation in 1974 with headquarters established in London under an outstanding statistician, Maurice (later Sir Maurice) Kendall. It was funded primarily by UNFPA and USAID. Its primary activity was the organization of sample surveys of fertility in ldcs: the design of questionnaires and samples for each country, selection and training of interviewers, oversight of the conduct of the survey, and participation in its analysis. The surveys were conducted in forty-two less–developed countries; they provided the richest and best quality comparative data available by the early 1980s on the demography of the third world.

I became involved in the design and analysis of the World Fertility Surveys, serving on several committees and making eleven trips to London to visit the headquarters on Grosvenor Gardens. These trips gave Sue and me a very pleasant exposure to London. We located a nice small comfortable hotel in Knightsbridge; it was a colorful walk for me to the WFS office; we ate well in small restaurants we found; in the morning or evening I could take a stroll around the lake in Hyde Park; we sampled the London theater; and we (especially Sue) enjoyed the marvelous London museums.

The most colorful experience we had with the WFS was a trip to Nepal (with a visit to Shri Lanka thrown in). The WFS design for the Nepal Survey began with a staff visit to Nepal in 1975; the survey itself was conducted in 1976; the Country Report was published in 1977; a national meeting was scheduled for the presentation of the report in Katmandhu in 1978. Sir Maurice Kendall was invited to this meeting to represent the London headquarters and its role in designing and analyzing the Nepal Survey. I was invited to represent technical demography, both in noting (and where possible correcting) such biases as misreported ages, and in interpreting the reported levels and trends of fertility, nuptiality, and mortality.

Sir Maurice and Lady Kendall came to Katmandhu from London; Sue and I from Bankok where the NAS Committee panel on Thailand had met. Both couples arrived several days before the scheduled meeting. The government provided a car, a driver, and a junior official as guide, to take the four visitors to Pokhara, within sight of the very high Himalayas. We drove over high passes into this smaller city, but found the mountains obscured by mist. We went for a ride in a small boat on a beautiful lake, and in the middle of this ride the mist lifted and we had a clear view of one of the highest peaks. The next day we were scheduled to fly back to Katmandhu. When we arrived at the airport the flight was canceled because of poor visibility en route. So in the government car with our guide we set out on the long drive to the capital. As we drove along we heard a loud bang and developed a bumpy ride. I got out on the left side, went back and found the left rear tire totally flat. With lots of experience over many years in changing tires, I found a jack and proceeded to remove the wheel with the flat. Maurice appeared on the right side of the car, and said I was removing the wrong wheel: the flat tire was on the right rear wheel. There were two flat tires! There was only one spare; we were stranded. We flagged down a large truck headed in our direction. There were two or three men in seats in the cab behind the driver; they moved into the cargo area along with our car driver, who carried the left rear wheel with its flat tire. His mission was to ride to the next gas station, have the tire repaired or replaced and make his way back to the car. (The spare could be put on the right rear wheel). The truck was not going to Katmandhu, but was stopping at a crossroads where there was no hotel and certainly no taxis. It was essential for us to be back that evening because our meeting was scheduled for the next morning, and members of the royal family were to be present. There was a public bus parked nearby; the resourceful guide persuaded the driver to take us back to our hotel in the capital for a price that he negotiated. When we stopped at a barrier for a government inspection, a bystander asked if we were going to Katmandhu, and then got aboard. The bus driver's assistant collected a fare from this additional passenger.

When the four of us (the extra passenger having disembarked) arrived at our respectable hotel in a forty passenger bus, I thought we would attract attention. Instead the porter took our luggage and remarked "You are already registered, I believe." (I had not finished with Nepal. In 1979, I coauthored with Noreen Goldman and Max Weinstein WFS Scientific Report #6, *The Quality of Data in the Nepal Fertility Survey*).

We went from Katmandhu to Colombo, Sri Lanka, for a national meeting for the presentation of the WFS report on Sri Lanka. We enjoyed the visit, had an audience with the President to discuss population in Sri Lanka, but had no double flat tires or strange bus rides.

Activities Related to China and its Population

In telling about my work with the NAS Committee on Population and Demography, I described the report on the population of China published by the committee, and the earlier activities that led me to write the report. I turn now to a further account of these activities.

In 1980 I was invited (by the UN Fund for Population Activities, at the request of the government of China) to make a visit to China, during which I would give a series of lectures on demography at the Peoples' University, meet with government officials and other persons concerned with strengthening demographic research, with the assembling and distribution of demographic data, and the formation and execution of population policies. I went to the UN headquarters to be briefed for the trip. I explained that I did not need instructions on demographic lectures; I did need one piece of information, the name of the hotel in Beijing where we were to stay. Friends who had gone to China said that on arrival they had to know in which hotel they held a reservation; when they went without a reservation to a hotel whose name they knew, they were not accepted, and much confusion reigned until the problem was solved. I was told not to worry; the UN representative in Beijing was getting our itinerary, and we would be met at the airport. When we arrived at the airport we found no one who spoke English, much less someone to meet us. We found our luggage, went to the exit from the waiting room: still no English speakers. I remembered that a colleague who had visited the Peoples' University had stayed at the Friendship Hotel. We finally conveyed to a taxi driver that we wanted to go to the Friendship. When we arrived at the hotel, the clerk did not speak English and could find no record of a reservation. A resourceful bell captain put us in contact with an English speaking government official. His job was to host the foreign visitors who came to China to teach in various programs. He got us assigned a room reserved for his foreign charges, and got us admitted to the dining room for dinner. He must also have gotten in contact with the university, because at about nine o'clock two agitated professors showed up at our room. They had been told by the UN representative in Beijing that we were due on the next day, but that the flight number and arrival time were not known. (The UN had arranged our flight and its travel agent had issued the tickets). The university had arranged to meet the next day all of the arriving planes with US connections. As I commented earlier, routine arrangements are not a strong point in the United Nations.

Before leaving the United States for China, I had asked how the consecutive translation of my 15 three hour lectures was to be handled. I was told that the Chinese would provide a translator. I envisioned a professional interpreter from the foreign office, who would be bilingual, but would not know the subject. He would surely mistranslate many technical points, and I would never know it. I telephoned Honolulu and found that Chi Tsien Tuan, at the East-West Population Institute, would be willing to serve as translator, and that the Center would grant him paid leave, but would not cover his travel. I knew that my expenses were to be paid (as budgeted) by China out of a UNFPA grant. The Chinese demurred about paying Tuan's travel costs, since they planned other uses for the money from the UN. The Rockefeller Foundation responded to an emergency appeal by paying for a round trip air fare from Honolulu to Beijing. Tuan was invaluable as the interpreter; he had done graduate work in Princeton and London, was the author of several excellent professional articles, and was a native of China. Several times when I was discussing a difficult point, he would stop his translation and say: "Would you repeat the last sentence?" I learned that on many evenings some of those attending the lectures would go to Tuan's room in the hotel to get clarification of things they had not understood.

I gave the promised 15 three hour lectures in three weeks at the People's University to an audience of some 60 persons from 12 universities and various government agencies. I covered more than half of the material given in two one-semester graduate courses at Princeton. The Chinese did not have the advantage the Princeton students enjoy (?) of several hours of preparation for each lecture.

While we were living in the Friendship Hotel, Professor Wu of People's University and Mrs. Wu treated us to some guided sightseeing and other pleasant diversions (such as attending a Chinese opera). Both of the Wus had studied in the US and spoke fluent English. As we got better acquainted, our hosts began to make some generally cautious remarks about life in China. The Cultural Revolution had ended recently, and the "Gang of Four" had recently been denounced. One of the first subtle indications of dissatisfaction was holding up one finger when mentioning the Gang of Four. One night we had a late dinner on the top floor of the Friendship Hotel, as I recall to see the telecast of my audience with the Vice Premier. The Wus told us a little of their experience during the Cultural Revolution. They had been charged with no disloyalty, but as members of the intellectual class, they were sent to the country to work on a cooperative farm and learn from the peasants. The professor was sent north and his wife south, not to see each other until the cultural revolution was over. Their sons were sent to still different places of exile. A

mathematician friend was denied access to pencil and paper lest he inter-
rupt his learning from the peasants by doing some mathematics.

In addition to lecturing at Peoples' University, I met with academics
at other universities, and with many government officials including the
Vice Premier in charge of family planning, the vice president of the Chinese Academy of Social Sciences (and other members of the Academy),
the acting director of the census, and the vice minister of education and
his staff. In all of these meetings (which included several banquets), I emphasized a list of actions necessary to improve the level of demographic
expertise and the basis for formulating and executing optimal population
policy. These suggestions included publication of detailed data from the
censuses of 1953 and 1964, inclusion in the next census of many special
questions such as a listing of deaths in the household in the year before
the census by age and sex of the decedent, and the initiation of sample
surveys both at the national level by the government, and on a smaller
scale by the population centers at universities. When I returned to the
United States I wrote a thirty page report to the UNFPA describing
the content of my lectures, listing the people with whom I had talked, and
making a systematic statement of the recommendations I had made. I feel
sure that this report was forwarded to China.

On rereading the report, I am struck by how almost every step I included in my recommendations corresponds with what has actually happened. The 1982 census did include detailed data from the 1953 and 1964
censuses, did incorporate questions on children ever born and number
surviving, and on deaths in 1981 in each household classified by age and
sex of the decedent, etc. In 1982 a very large sample survey was conducted
by the State Family Planning Commission, a survey covering households
with a total of more than a million inhabitants. This survey brings together the life histories of more than 300,000 women at ages 15 to 67, including the woman's date of birth, date of marriage, date of birth of each
child and whether the child is still alive at the date of the survey.

When the 1982 fertility survey was being planned, a team from the
Family Planning Commission came to the United States to get expert advice on the design and conduct of a survey in this field. They obtained
substantial help in designing the sample from Leslie Kish at the University of Michigan, and visited several university-based demographic research centers plus the UN and the US Bureau of the Census. They spent
two days at the Office of Population Research talking to Charles Westoff,
Norman Ryder, and myself. Ryder and Westoff had been pioneers in survey research on fertility in the United States and had been principal authors of the core questionnaire of the World Fertility Survey. They made

many suggestions about the wording of questions concerning contraceptive practice, intentions about future childbearing, etc. I remember insisting that dates of events (such as the birth and the marriage of the respondent, and the birth of each of her children) be asked in the Chinese lunar calendar, and later be translated, perhaps by computer, into the western calendar. Then these western dates could be subtracted from the date of the survey to obtain precise measures of age and duration. One of the visitors said that since the Revolution, Chinese respondents could supply accurate western dates. I replied perhaps in the large cities, but not in remote rural areas. After the mission from China had spent two days in discussion with us, they left for Washington and consultation with the Census Bureau. Charlie, Norm, and I spent several hours putting our suggestions in writing (including a redrafted questionnaire) and sent them to the Chinese visitors in care of the Census.

One or two years later, I attended a seminar on the large scale fertility survey at the East-West Center in Honolulu. I recognized the head of the mission that had visited Princeton, and asked him if they had received our written recommendations before they left Washington. He said they certainly had. In fact the text had been translated into Chinese and a copy sent to every sampling point. "That's probably the biggest circulation you ever had!" he added.

Since composing the NAS report on China using the burst of data that began emerging in 1982, I have continued my interest in Chinese population trends, attending three conferences, including a large assembly devoted to the 1990 census, held in Beijing in 1992. It was very pleasing to have a number of the Chinese participants tell me that they had attended my lectures at Peoples' University 12 years earlier. I have also been involved in further research on the demography of China, writing more than ten articles or monographs, some in collaboration with Chinese visitors, or with colleagues at Michigan, the East-West Population Institute, or the Center for International Research at the Census Bureau.

Participation in the International Union for the Scientific Study of Population and in International Conferences

The IUSSP is an organization mostly of professional demographers. Its purpose is primarily the advancement of research in demography and the dissemination of scientific knowledge on population. Its title is a reflection of the intention of its founders to make it clear that the Union was not an organization advocating causes, such as birth control or eugenics. It has held 22 international conferences, the most recent in Montreal in 1993. I began attending these meetings in the 1950s.

My especially close involvement in the IUSSP began in 1973 at the quadrennial meeting held in Liege, Belgium. Before this meeting I was in Florence and had a conversation with Massimo Livy-Bacci, who was then the secretary-treasurer of the Union. He asked me if I would object if the committee on nominations were to enter my name as a candidate for vice president. He explained that the vice president served for four years on the Council of the Union and then automatically succeeded to the presidency. I understood this sequence, but thought that the election process in the Union was similar to that in the Population Association of America. In the PAA, the nominating committee proposes at least two names for each position, and the membership selects the winners by a popular vote. I assumed that there would be at least one other nominee for vice president, and that there was enough anti-American sentiment to insure my defeat. Some other activity made me miss the general assembly where the vote took place. I was walking by the door when the meeting ended, and a friend told me that I (the only candidate of the nominating committee) had been elected vice president. I returned to our hotel room to give the news to Sue, telling her how depressed I was because I would have to attend meetings of the IUSSP council for four years as vice president and then have executive responsibility as president for four more. I said that I was already the Director of the Office of Population Research, and Chairman of the NAS Committee on Population, responsible for two organizations with large annual budgets. I said that I had entered academia to teach and to do stimulating research, not for administrative work. Now I faced eight years of an additional administrative load! "Maybe you won't live that long," was Sue's consoling response. Actually I am still alive 26 years later. In fact, I enjoyed the meetings of the Council and the warm friendships I made, especially with the paid administrative staff, under the executive secretary, Bruno Remiche, but also with the diverse members of the Council (in 1977 eight members from eight countries).The council meetings were held in Liege, where the Union had rented a building to serve as its headquarters. We got to know the restaurants and the rather thin list of tourist attractions in Liege in weak analogy to the chance to know London from WFS meetings.

One memorable adventure took place while I was serving as president. Before a scheduled meeting of the Council, Bruno Remiche asked me in a phone call whether I would like to fly to Paris on the Concorde. I replied that I would not pay the extravagant one-way fare, nor would I agree to its being paid by the IUSSP. Bruno then told me that Mr. Leynen, who made travel arrangements for the Union, did such a large volume of business with Air France that the airline had offered passage on the Concord for tourist fare. I gladly accepted the offer. When I reached the Air France terminal at JFK, I was ushered into the special Concord waiting room, where champagne and hors d'oeuvres were served. A hostess approached and asked could she take my coat and hand luggage. I said that it was not necessary, since we would soon board, and she replied that she would return the items to me when we arrived in Paris. Not like tourist class! When we reached the airport in Paris (at 6 PM, New York time, but 11 PM, in France), I found that a hotel room was being held for me. I was to fly to Brussels the next morning. Since it was only 6 PM, for me, and since I had feasted on the plane, I entered the hotel bar to have a night cap. There was one other customer and one bartender present. I was asked what was my next stop, and replied "Bruxelles." "Pommes frites," commented the bartender. I then explained that two of my best friends were Belgian: Etienne and Francine Van de Walle. They had come to America to study and work at the Office of Population Research, and had brought their young children with them. When they arrived in America, their children enrolled in public schools and by the end of the first year were speaking without a trace of an accent, although their parents, despite about 30 years of distinguished professional careers in American universities, still have a noticeable trace of foreign origin in their speech. The family returned to Francine's parental home outside Brussels every summer when the children were young. I related these facts at the bar, and concluded that the children were very fortunate to be bilingual in French and English. "You mean in Belgian and American," said the bartender.

My term as president of the IUSSP ended at the quadrennial conference held in Manila in 1981. The formal opening session was addressed by President Marcos in a large auditorium, filled as much with Phillipino supporters of Marcos as with IUSSP members. As the meeting was to start, Marcos and I walked down the aisle to the stage together, with everyone standing and applauding. He gave an interesting and witty address with no manuscript or notes on the podium. There were large bullet–proof transparent plastic screens between the speaker and the audience; standing behind Marcos I could see that the text of his speech was projected on these screens by some kind of side illumination that produced words visible to the speaker but not to the audience. He could glance from right to left as he chose and "extemporize" by reading from the screens.

In our informal conversation he asked where I was from. When I said Princeton, he remarked that his daughter was enrolled there as a student. Later he asked if I were going straight home after the conference. I explained that I was stopping a few days in Honolulu for consultation at the East-West population institute, and that Sue planned to go to the beach with old friends while I was consulting. When we exited the auditorium together he went to the waiting limousine, and turned to say goodbye. "Have a pleasant trip home, and a productive visit to the East-West center. I hope your wife enjoys the beach."

Only a skilled politician would thus remember our casual conversation!

I have presented papers at at least six of the IUSSP general Conferences, and have also been involved in two World population conferences sponsored by the United Nations (with IUSSP participation). The UN sponsored a world conference on population, of a scientific nature, held in Rome in 1954. The participants were invited as individuals, and no resolutions (only summaries of discussions) were published. The second World Population Conference, with similar purposes and principles of organization, was held with UN sponsorship in Belgrade in 1965. I gave a paper summarizing the exploratory work on the European fertility project at the Belgrade Conference.

The next World Population Conference organized by the United Nations, in Bucharest in 1974, was not a meeting of experts to discuss technical subjects, but a meeting of government representatives to discuss population policy, with a document, "The World Population Plan of Action," as a basis of the discussion.

A draft World Plan of Action was prepared with the assistance of an advisory committee of experts and the Population Commission. It was discussed with government representatives in regional consultations in Latin America, South East Asia, Africa, West Asia, and Europe. The draft plan contained such liberal provisions as recognition of the right of every couple to make an informed choice about the number and spacing of children. It had had the active support of the US representative on the Population Commission.

The US delegation to the 1974 Conference in Bucharest was composed largely of enthusiastic advocates of reduced fertility, and of international steps to stimulate lower fertility in less developed countries. The delegation did not include any professional demographers, and just before the conference began, I was added as a senior advisor. As the conference was opening, our delegation was proposing that the world plan of action be modified to require every country to set a target for the level of fertility to be attained by 1985. This last minute addition to the plan of action was directly counter to a position that was gathering strength among delegates from the Soviet Bloc, and from many of the countries in Latin America and Africa. This position was that the problems in the LDCs were the result of inadequate economic development originating in colonialism and capitalist exploitation, and that the conference should concentrate on development rather than contraception. Two slogans were often repeated. "Development is the best contraceptive," and "Take care of the people, and the population will take care of itself." The US strong stand on reducing fertility, including the call for a specific fertility target in each country in 1985, was abrasive in this context. For example, the delegation from India withdrew its support for the World Plan of Action. Friends of mine from the international community of demographers, such as Mick Borrie of Australia, asked what was going on in the US delegation.

I asked the head of the delegation to be allowed to speak at a private meeting of the US group. I pointed out that some of our positions were hypocritical, since neither the congress nor the president would follow the recommendation to set a numerical target for US fertility. I felt that taking such a position was weakening support for the good provisions of the plan of action. Actually I have since concluded that while the actions taken by the conference watered down the draft plan of action, the net effect of the conference was to accelerate the development of national support of family planning programs in LDCs, because the participation of government officials from these countries brought population problems to their conscious attention.

At the same time the conference was meeting, there was a nongovernmental group called the Population Tribune meeting separately. Made up of members of non governmental organizations and private individuals interested in population, the Tribune took no actions, but discussed many of the issues faced by the conference. An almost dominant subject for discussion was the view that what the world needed was a new economic order, rather than a world plan of action for population. I recall two minor episodes with respect to this topic. John D. Rockefeller gave a speech to the Tribune in which, reflecting the influence of Joan Dunlop, a new advisor on population, he recommended more attention to economic and social factors rather than the mere promotion of contraception. After he had finished a young LDC radical asked for the floor, and started: "Mr. Rockefeller, how can you say that it is not development policy that matters but birth control?" Carmen Miro was in the chair, and interrupted by saying: "You did not listen. Sit down!" The other episode was an intervention by Paul Demeny in reaction to demands that the conference should discuss development rather than population. He said he

could picture a world conference on transportation in which delegates insisted that the control of nuclear weapons was more important than
transportation, and weapons control is what should be discussed. He
agreed that economic development is very important, but felt it appropriate to discuss population at a population conference.

Visiting Activity at Other Academic Institutions

Over an interval of many years I made one or two visits each year to
the East-West Population Institute in Honolulu. In the fall of 1978 I spent
part of a fall term leave of absence at the Population Institute; my other
visits were usually during the Christmas or summer vacation periods. I
remember arriving at the beginning of the Christmas holiday period and
hearing a colleague remark "It must be Christmas time, Coale is here."
"Yes," replied another, "and the computer staff will be tied up for the next
couple of weeks." The Institute has been a very stimulating environment
because of the several talented and congenial professional staff members
with whom I have worked, the well run library, the presence of other visitors like Ron Freedman, the extensive inventory of machine readable
data especially from China and Korea, and the talented and productive
staff of computer programmers. We have personally profited from the
features of Hawaii that make it a famous resort. In some of our longer
stays, we rented a nice cottage on a lonely sector of beach, a private house
in a quiet neighborhood, and an apartment belonging to a colleague who
was away. In more recent years we have taken a room in a hotel on a beach
patronized mostly by local residents, and at the far end of an uncrowded
public park. From our room in this hotel we can watch the spectacular
tropical sunset. I ride a rented bicycle the three miles up to the East-West
center after a before-breakfast swim along the beach. Sue had found some
old friends (including the former professor at UCLA and his wife, from
whom we had rented a house in West Los Angeles in the early 1950s),
friends with whom she walked on beaches far from the hotel, and who
guided her to such places as the better local museums.

I have twice served as a visiting professor in demography: for one semester at Berkeley in 1987, and for one month at the University of Rome
in 1990. In Berkeley, I taught a regular second semester graduate course
in technical demography, and supervised the research of several of the advanced students. I was given an office in the small ex-private house in
which the graduate program in population studies is located. It was very
agreeable to work in an office surrounded by very congenial and brilliant
colleagues and the grad students. One day as lunchtime approached, the

chairman, Gene Hammell, said that he wished to hold a meeting of the faculty, and invited me to attend. A very small group gathered around a table. Hammell announced that we would have to wait for the secretary to bring the agenda. I tried to pass the time by raising a question about English usage. I frequently told my students that data is a plural word (the singular is datum), and it seemed to me that agenda was also plural. In Latin the verb to do is *ago agere egi actus*, of which the singular gerundive is *agendum*, something that must be done. The plural is *agenda*, things that must be done. Yet no one (not even the British Parliament) seems to ask "What are the agenda?" At this point Gene Hammell asked "What is the plural of pedantic?"

Our friends had found us a wonderful house in Berkeley to rent, perhaps a mile and a half from the office. It was on the side of the steep hill that rises above the Bay in Berkeley, and had a view out through the Golden Gate as well as across to San Francisco, from the study in the basement and the porch on the first floor to the picture window in the main bedroom on the second floor. I had bought a bicycle and rode to work each day up and down the steep inclines along the way. Traveling down hill one morning at probably 25 miles per hour, I caught the front tire in a tarry slot, yanked on the handle bar, and soared over it to land on my head. Fortunately I had bought a sturdy plastic helmet; it was cracked; in its absence my skull would have surely been crushed. I was wearing a bag over my shoulder in which I carried a husky steel cable to lock the bike. Carried over by momentum I was severely bruised in my back by this cable. Picking myself up and waving off the motorist who had stopped to help if needed, I decided to walk back to the house and ask Sue to drive me to the office. When I first stood up I could not remember where the house was, so I simply started back uphill as the right direction, and by the end of the block I remembered how to go. Sue took me to a hospital on the campus and a very nice female doctor took x-rays in the area of the bruises on my back. I was told to return after the x-rays had been developed. When I reentered the waiting room, gave my name, and sat down, the attendant called "Ansley." I went to the desk and reported that I had an appointment with Helen. On my next visit I was addressed as "Professor Coale." I do not object to being addressed by my first name by my graduate students, but I knew that the medical attendant would never use a doctor's first name, and that to use mine was condescending. The bruise was painful but not serious; I did not miss a class, although the quality of my instruction may have suffered.

In the winter of 1990 I was invited to be for a month a visiting professor at the University of Rome, in the special program in demography. I spent the month on a special research project in collaboration with Professoressa Graziella Caselli. The project was to develop a method for ascertaining the accurate distribution by age for the population over 70 (when the ages of the elderly are misreported) from the accurately recorded ages at death in three consecutive years. (In several European countries the ages of the very old are misreported in censuses, but deaths are completely registered and with precise ages at death). Graziella and I worked quite intensively each day from the hour when the office opened until I had to leave to meet Sue for dinner. Our job was to enter relevant data from different countries in a desk computer and run a program that we developed to see whether our methods worked. I read the numbers and Graziella entered them in the machine. Our communication was in Italian, and after a month of this intense work my command of the spoken language was more fluent than ever before; indeed I gave three lectures in Italian, in Rome, Florence, and Padua. Our visit to Rome for this brief professorship was especially enjoyable for Sue and me. We had spent two one–semester leaves in Rome, in 1959 and 1963, and had lots of favorite places to revisit or to dine in again. Graziella and her husband Marco were congenial good company. They took us into the hill country in the south of Tuscany one weekend; I was embarrassed when entering a beautiful church in a small village to remember that Sue and I had seen it earlier when making a scenic trip between the Rome airport and Florence.

We had exceptional living conditions in Rome because a good friend of ours in Princeton (the wife of a professor) had been a generous donor to the American Academy in Rome, in support of archeological work in Greece. When she heard of our prospective sojourn, she suggested we might want to stay in quarters the Academy maintained for visitors. The result was that we spent a month in a lovely apartment in a building across the street from the headquarters of the American Academy, a top floor apartment with a kitchen, a bath, two bedrooms, and a 40-foot living room with a long window giving a view (from our hill top location) of classical Rome across the Tiber. I walked a couple of hundred yards to a bus stop, took a bus (no fare for a person over 65) to near the railroad terminal, and then walked maybe a half mile to the office where I worked at the University of Rome.

I became a foreign advisor to the Pakistan Institute of Development Economics in 1969 when it was in Karachi, gave a pair of lectures in 1989, the eighth in a series in development economics, and participated in the seventh annual general meeting in 1991. The Institute has become a leader in economics in Pakistan (indeed in South Asia) and has done much to stimulate good research in demography. In addition to giving lectures there, I have served as a referee for the Pakistan Development Review.

Two adventures were my lot in my most recent visits to Islamabad. One involved the disposition of the honorarium for my lecture, which was paid in Pakistani currency, not convertible into dollars. I knew that Pakistani oriental rugs were especially beautiful, so I asked a demographer on the staff of the Institute if she knew where I might find a nice choice at modest prices. She replied that her husband ran a shop that sold beautiful rugs. With their help in the choice, I bought two exceptionally beautiful carpets at a privileged price. The second adventure involved my careless departure from the tight rules about diet I follow when traveling in the third world. The Institute of Development Economics had housed its guests in a luxurious hotel where the water was pure and the meals scrupulously safe. We had had delicious meals, usually together with the officials from the Institute. The day before our departure, some of the younger Pakistani at the conference offered to take me to a good local restaurant to sample the native cuisine. I had a delicious meal, and, engrossed in the conversation, I drank a full glass of water. The next day I went to the local airport to fly to Karachi, to make connections with a Swissair flight to continue around the world, permitting a stopover in Honolulu to visit the East-West center and join Sue. At the airport in Islamabad I was escorted to the VIP lounge from where at departure time a private car took me to the plane on the landing strip.

When I arrived at the Karachi Airport I was again taken to the VIP lounge, told that my check-in with Swissair was being taken care of, to rest on the sofa, that I would be wakened and taken to the plane. Again, after the plane had loaded, I was taken in a private car to the ramp which led to the first–class entrance to the plane. I felt conspicuous as I walked back through first class to my seat in tourist. I was glad it was Swissair; the glass of water caught up with me and I spent most of the flight to Hong Kong in the toilet. When I arrived in Honolulu, I found a clinic that specialized in tropical dysentery, and was given effective medicine.

TEACHING AND RELATION TO STUDENTS

MY EXPERIENCE IN TEACHING began when as an undergraduate I undertook the job as student tutor for the introductory course in psychology. I engaged in very little individual tutoring; usually I gave three-hour review sessions, one before each mid-term hour test, and two before each final examination. I gained experience in summarizing and clarifying and in answering questions, a useful background for my later teaching in the Radar school run by MIT for training army, navy, and air force officers during World War II.

I have always enjoyed teaching, including the early experiences just mentioned and later courses in such subjects as statistics, mathematical economics, and international trade, when I served as an assistant professor at Princeton beginning in 1947. Most rewarding has been teaching the undergraduate and graduate courses in demography, and supervising research on population matters since 1958, when Notestein resigned from Princeton to become president of the Population Council. More than 35 doctoral dissertations and more than 90 research papers by visiting graduate students have been prepared under my supervision. In many instances the dissertations have been undertaken to resolve an unanswered question that has arisen in my own research. I described earlier Alvaro Lopez's proof of a conjecture of mine that the age distribution of any population (not just of a stable population) is independent of the remote past. It was a hunch that I could support by arithmetical examples, but could not prove. Another example of a brilliant student's completing something I had started was Sam Preston's dissertation.

When constructing the Regional Model Life Tables, we built on the high intercorrelations between the death rates at different ages found within each of the four clusters of mortality schedules that serve as the basis of the four sets of "regional" model tables. We noted that the intercorrelations among rates at different ages were lower for male mortality than for female mortality, especially for correlations between rates at high and low ages. Analysis including as a variable the date of each mortality rate showed that male mortality (but not female mortality) at higher ages was relatively elevated at later dates. Preston showed that the excess–male mortality rates at the older ages at later dates is very tightly related to the per capita consumption of cigarettes.

My association with graduate students has been enriched by their brilliance and admirable character. Both qualities are shown by the fact that among the ten most recent presidents of the Population Association of America, five had been my students. The high distinction of demographers trained at Princeton is not, I must admit, primarily the result of the training we give, or even of the attraction of our demography program. Many of our best students have entered Princeton to study economics, sociology, or statistics, and decided to include population in their studies only after their arrival. The median score on the graduate record exams of students admitted to the PhD program in economics was at one point at the 95th percentile. Students of this quality make good demographers.

Al Hermalin is a student who did come to Princeton specifically to study demography. He had graduated from college about 15 years before he entered graduate work at Princeton; he had worked as an actuary and craved more creative intellectual work. He published an excellent paper while a graduate student and subsequently has been an outstanding demographer at Michigan, serving as director of the Population Studies Center, and as president of the PAA. Al Hermalin deserves special mention because he embodies the quality in addition to brilliance found in our students: an admirable character. He embodies perhaps the highest levels of generosity and honesty I have ever known. His son Ben came to Princeton as an undergraduate. I got to know him well because while an undergraduate he took the two basic courses in demography and worked as a brilliant research assistant at the OPR. While Ben was here, Al returned on a professional appointment. One day I said to Ben that his father was the most consistently benign person that I knew. Ben thought a minute and said "I agree with that." How many children would say that of a parent?

The personal as well as intellectual ties that developed between me and the students I have supervised is illustrated by Pravin Visaria's experience while a student at Princeton and later. Visaria came to the university in the late 1950s as a visiting student in demography. He did very well in his course work, and was accepted as a PhD candidate in economics. When he had passed his general exams and was to continue in residence to write a dissertation, he came to me with a personal problem. When he had left India his parents had thought his stay was to be one year as a visitor, and were somewhat upset at his stay for two years to take his PhD exams. He said that his father was insisting that he return to India before starting further work in America. I told Pravin that I sympathized with his problem, and would favor permitting the postponement of his thesis work until the end of the summer. I added that since his return was for personal reasons, I could not recommend that the Population Council, which had agreed to extend his fellowship while he worked on his thesis, should support his return trip. He said the expenses would not be a problem; returning with an MA from Princeton and the likelihood of a doctorate, he could command a large dowry. Contrary to his expectations, when he returned to India, he fell in love with a young female sociologist who had graduated from Bombay. Some years after he had written a thesis on the ratio of males to females in the censuses of India (which was later published as an official report of the Census of India), he was invited back to the OPR as a research assistant. Leela accompanied him as a staff member's wife, and began informally to attend graduate courses in demography and sociology. She did so well that she was accepted as a PhD candidate in sociology, was awarded a Population Council Fellowship, and finished successfully with a valuable dissertation on religious and regional differences in fertility in India.

Later Pravin and Leela both held professional jobs in Washington. When their stay in the capital was over, Sue and I invited them to stay overnight at our house on their way to the New York airport when returning to India. They arrived on Saturday evening. I always prepare breakfast at our house, and I found the prospect of preparing a breakfast for the Visarias a problem. Not only vegetarians, they are Jains, who when the air is full of insects wear a cotton mask, not to prevent the discomfort of inhaling an insect but to protect the creatures from accidental death. I clearly could not serve eggs, much less any form of meat; I decided on hot biscuits and jam. When Pravin sampled the biscuits, he pronounced them delicious and completely within the Jain diet. "You will have to make these some time, Leela," he said. "Why should I make them?" she replied. The feminism of her fellow graduate students had had an effect on this Asian lady.

One aspect of my association with graduate students that they may well not appreciate is my compulsive correction of what I perceive to be incorrect English usage. One example is treatment of "data" as a singular noun. Another is what I regard as misuse of "hopefully." I contend that this word should appear in a sentence only when there is a noun or pronoun in the same sentence that does the hoping. Thus "Hopefully, I predict that the weather will be better tomorrow" is OK, but "Hopefully, the weather will be better tomorrow" is not. I used to illustrate the argument by the example that one can say "Regrettably, it is going to rain," but not "Regretfully, it is going to rain." When Preston went to Berkeley after receiving his PhD, in his first letter he wrote "Hopeably, everything is going well."

Another aspect of my teaching (indeed of my character) is a compulsion to tell jokes. I no longer remember the names, and sometimes even the faces, of old friends. I lose books and manuscripts, and forget my schedule. What I remember is jokes, especially those I heard many years ago. One of my friends told me that some former students were speculating about how many jokes I knew, and one surmised about 200. Asked how he arrived at that figure, he answered "By the capture-recapture method."

Recently I attended a memorial service at Pennsylvania for Anouche Chahnazarian, a former student of mine whose tragic death occurred in the early stage of an extraordinarily productive and versatile career. All of her colleagues and students marveled both at her brilliance and her wonderful personal qualities. I had been asked to be one of the speakers at the informal occasion, and I remarked that the most rewarding feature of teaching demography at the graduate level had been, for me, the intellectual and personal interaction with my students.

$\mathcal{R}$ECENT FORTUITOUS CONDITIONS FOR A DEMOGRAPHER

IN THE TWENTIETH CENTURY (especially the second half) there have been unique aspects in the development of the human population and in demography, its scientific study. There has been an unprecedented emergence of detailed and generally reliable data about the numbers and characteristics of persons and about the vital events to which they are subject in populations throughout the world. Many centers (government, international and academic centers) of demographic studies have been established. In this section I shall comment on some of these propitious circumstances in which I have been fortunate enough to work.

A Unique High Rate of Increase of the World Population

In the late seventeenth or early–eighteenth century there began a gradual acceleration in the rate of increase of the human population from the very low average rate that had been experienced from the earliest days of mankind. The acceleration increased in the nineteenth century and into the twentieth, especially after WWII. The annual rate reached a peak of 2 percent in the 1960s, and fell to about 1.7 percent in the late 1970s and through the early 1990s.

The fall in the growth rate from its peak of 2 percent to the recent rate of about 1.7 percent will surely resume and must continue until the rate is again close to zero within at most two or three hundred years. If the growth rate were to decline along a straight line from 2 percent in the 1960s to a future plateau at about zero annual growth, the average rate of increase during the period of decline would be 1 percent. At an annual average rate of increase of 1 percent, the 1990 population of 5.3 billion would reach over 14 billion in one century, 39 billion in two centuries, and more than 100 billion in three. The acceleration of the average increase from near zero to a peak rate of 2 percent lasted no more than three centuries; the return to an average rate near zero can inevitably take little longer. Hence if a person should look back from a date 1000 years into the future on the long history of population growth rates, the increase from near zero in the seventeenth century to the peak of 2 percent in the 1960s and then the return to near zero would look like a brief steep blip above the long term essentially horizontal trend—a unique blip.

The Mechanism of the Modern Rise and Fall of the Rate of Population Growth: The Demographic Transition

A model of the mechanism underlying the increase in the growth rate of a particular population, the attainment of a peak, and subsequent decline is given the name of the "demographic transition." In simplest terms, a population not yet affected by the social changes named modernization, is in the first stage of the transition: a stage of very gradual growth resulting from nearly equal and nearly constant (on average, possibly subject to substantial transient variation) high birth and death rates. Then a population that starts to undergo some particular effects of modernization enters the second stage of the transition: the beginning of a sustained decline in mortality while fertility remains at the earlier high level. In the third stage of the transition, a continued drop in mortality is combined with the initiation of a sustained decline in fertility. In the fourth stage a continued drop in the rate of childbearing together with the attainment of a quite high expectation of life lead to a period with a modest rate of increase.

The demographic transition began earlier in Western Europe and the overseas areas settled by western Europeans than in Asia, Africa, and Latin America; earlier in the more developed than in the less developed countries.

The second stage (the beginning of a sustained decline in death rates) began in Western Europe and Northern America in the seventeenth or eighteenth century. The causes of the initial improvements in survival rates are not easily specified. A popular hypothesis that improved diets played a major role is inconsistent with records showing a decline in the average stature of military recruits during this period. There are few recorded improvements in medicine except the development in the late–eighteenth century of a vaccine against smallpox, and its subsequent use. There is evidence of improvement in personal sanitation such as washing hands and occasional bathing. By the mid–nineteenth century, clean water supplies and sewage disposal became available in an increasing number of cities. In the twentieth century the rise in expectation of life in the mdc's became more rapid, with improvements in the treatment of infectious disease, the development of new vaccines, and further improvements in sanitation. Especially rapid increases occurred since 1930, with the discovery and use of sulfa drugs and antibiotics.

In most of the mdc's the level of fertility was only moderately high in the first stage of the transition, before modernization. The rate of child-bearing was restrained by late marriage and also permanent celibacy. In Western Europe in the eighteenth century the mean age at first marriage for women was between 23 and 28 years; the proportion of women still single at age 50 was 10 to 30 percent. Only about 50 percent of women of childbearing age were currently married. The recorded age pattern of marital fertility indicates that in the first and second stages in the mdc's, most married women did not deliberately stop childbearing by contra-ception or abortion after having borne a deliberately chosen number of babies. In the third stage in the mdc's (when a sustained decline in fertil-ity began) the practice of contraception and abortion spread through the population. In virtually every mdc, the total fertility rate fell by more than 50 percent from the early plateau, and has now reached a level insufficient to replace the parental generation. (The rate of natural increase is still positive in most of these countries because of large parental generations, born before fertility had fallen so low.)

The lag between the second and third stages (the earlier drop in mortality than in fertility in both mdc's and ldc's) is largely accounted for by the general desire for lower mortality in all populations, and the need for a change in attitudes before lower fertility is desired. There has been much speculation about the features of modernization that have caused the virtually universal decline in the rate of childbearing in the more de-veloped countries. When faced with scholars who express doubt about whether modernization inevitably leads to lower fertility, Livi-Bacci com-mented that if a population lives in apartment houses, and has radios, television sets, telephones, refrigerators, and automobiles, it never has an average of eight children per couple.

The second stage in the transition—a large decline in mortality, while fertility remains at or near traditional high levels—has occurred in all less developed countries. A few relatively advanced ldc's had attained a substantial increase in life expectancy by early in this century, but many of the countries with retarded development had an expectation of life at birth around 1930 no higher than had been attained before 1800 in West-ern Europe. This lag of the ldc's behind the mdc's of well over a century in attaining a given e_0 had been reduced to no more than 30 or 40 years by the 1980's. In other words, the decline in mortality in the ldc's was much later than the decline in the mdc's, but has also been much more rapid. The much more rapid decline in mortality was possible because the ldc's did not need to develop on their own the forces that led to lower death rates, but could import them from the mdc's. Indeed technical assistance in medicine and public health was provided by programs manned and funded by generous donor countries, by international agencies, and by private foundations.

The third stage of the transition (the beginning of a sustained decline in fertility) occurred as early as before 1800 in France, and among certain minorities in other European countries, such as segments of the aristocracy. It typically occurred in mdc's other than France between 1870 and 1930 and is now a universal part of the history of advanced countries. This stage has now been at least initiated in all ldcs' except some in tropical Africa and West Asia. In both more advanced and less advanced areas, the reduction in mortality preceded the drop in fertility. The change in attitudes before the rate of childbearing falls is not as readily transferred from the first world to the third as are effective means of curtailing mortality.

Expansion of Data on Population

National censuses of population and large scale registration of vital events originated at about the time that the rate of increase in the population of the world began to accelerate. Registration of births, deaths, and marriages in church parishes occurred in earlier centuries, and has made possible the recreation of records of population and vital statistics before national data were available (Wrigley and Schofield, 1981). The first national census was taken in Sweden in 1751. The US constitution required that a census be conducted every decade to allocate the number of members in the House of Representatives among the states; the first of the decennial series was taken in 1790. Censuses every ten years also began around 1800 in England and France. By 1900 regular censuses were conducted in most of the more developed countries, and in a few ldc's, most notably the sequence of decennial censuses of India beginning in 1871. Registration of births, deaths, and marriages began in Western Europe in the eighteenth century; in the United States the official registration areas for births and deaths did not include all of the states until after 1930; some omission of births and deaths from registration continued even after all states were in the official area.

By 1900 regular censuses were conducted in almost all of the more developed countries, and in a few less developed areas, most notably the sequence of decennial census that began in India in 1871. In this century the coverage and quality of demographic data has increased in synchronism with the rising rate of growth in the human population. The first census in what later became the Soviet Union was held in 1897. An important gap in population data was the absence of a census in Mainland China until 1953; the results of this census were not in fact published until 1982. There were virtually no reliable data on the population of Africa South of the Sahara (with the partial exception of the Union of South Africa) until after WWII. Since that time there have been attempted full enumerations covering nearly all of the world's populations, and the UN publishes some population data for essentially all member nations. The increasing scope of useful demographic data has been much enhanced by the invention and greatly expanded application of new methods for collecting, correcting, and analyzing demographic data.

Sample Surveys

A very useful innovation has been the collection of data from a sample of the population. This method has been used to compare information taken from a carefully selected sample with the data in the census for the whole population to verify and sometimes adjust the data in the full enumeration, and in other instances to infer the characteristics for the whole populations by inflation of results from the sample. A particularly valuable application of sample surveys is their use to collect information on human fertility.

The pioneering exercise was the Indianapolis Study, an investigation of the "social and psychological factors" affecting fertility, in a sample of married couples in Indianapolis, interviewed in 1940–1941. This survey was designed by a committee sponsored by the Millbank Memorial Fund and financed by the Carnegie Corporation. The aim was to extend the scope of fertility research to include information about contraceptive practice, desired family size, and the social, psychological, and economic characteristics of the parental couples. The findings were disappointing (someone referred to the "social and psychological factors *barely* affecting fertility") but the experience provided a foundation for an expanding universe of fertility survey research that is a principal source of our present scientific knowledge and fruitful ideas about population. In 1955 a national sample fertility survey was started by Freedman, Whelpton, and Campbell; and in 1957, the Princeton Fertility Survey was initiated as a conscious sequel to the Indianapolis study. It surveyed in eight metropolitan areas all of the women who had borne a second child in a specified month. (The names and addresses of the respondents were obtained from the birth certificates.) A particular asset of this project is that the respondents were reinterviewed three years and six years later, making it possible to compare intentions with subsequent behavior. The Princeton

Survey was succeeded by the National Fertility Survey in 1965 under the leadership of Westoff and Ryder. It was repeated in 1970 and 1975; in 1976 the government instituted the national survey of population growth, which has been conducted again in 1982, 1988, and 1983.

In recent years fertility surveys have been carried out throughout much of the world, and have greatly extended our knowledge of demographic statistics, especially in less developed countries. An international program of sample surveys, known as the World Fertility Survey, was initiated in 1971 in London under the direction of Sir Maurice Kendall within the International Statistical Institute, with financial support from the US Agency for International Development, the United Nations Fund for Population Activities, and other agencies. WFS was involved in the conduct of large scale surveys in about 40 ldc's. It helped in the design of each survey schedule, the design of the sample, and the selection, training, and supervision of the interviewers. Among the expert personnel who participated in this enterprise were Westoff and Ryder, who drew on their background of involvement in so much American fertility survey work.

As the World Fertility program was completed in 1984, a new set of fertility surveys was initiated at what is now the Institute for Resource Development with funds from USAID. This series, which includes surveys in 42 less developed countries, is known as the Demographic and Health Surveys. These two large international survey programs have supplied data on fertility, marriage, contraceptive practice, abortion, desired fertility, and maternal and child health for populations in Africa, Asia, and Latin America. There has been as great a relative peak in the growth in the availability of pertinent and useful demographic data as in the growth of the global population itself.

The Modern Growth in Population Studies

Another facet of demographic development has been the emergence of a science of population studies. It began at about the time that the acceleration in world population growth was initiated. The work often cited as the first modern demographic publication is John Graunt's "Natural and Political Observations . . . Made upon the Bills of Mortality" (1662). The Bills were current reports on burials (and christenings) of persons in the vicinity of London. In 1693 the astronomer Edmund Halley constructed the first empirical life table (for Breslau) from records of births and deaths. In the nineteenth century the development of analytical demography was rather gradual. In Malthus's 1824 edition of his essay on population, he showed (with the help of an actuary) that the age distribution in the United States in the first three US censuses was consistent with a rate of increase that doubled the number of persons every 25 years combined with a sensible estimate of the mortality schedule. The basic equation for this calculation had been stated by Euler in 1760, and the relation between mortality, growth and age distribution was to be precisely analyzed and set forth by Lotka after 1900. This early elegant analysis was not given much emphasis by Malthus and was not the subject of comment or further development until the following century.

The Growth of Population Studies in this Century

The analytical research that began in the seventeenth century with Graunt's "Observations on the Bills . . . ," and the calculation of the first life tables has ripened in the twentieth century into a fertile and useful science. One example is the introduction and increasing use of component projection. Component projection makes possible the calculation of the subsequent population implied by the population at a given moment, together with specified ensuing age schedules of fertility, mortality, and net migration. This art is analogous to the use by physicists of Newtonian laws of motion to calculate the trajectory of an object from data on its initial position and motion and the subsequent forces to which it is subject. Projections became the means for making provisional forecasts of future populations (provisional on the assumptions made about the determining variables). Now the UN Population Division, the World Bank, and the Bureau of the Census routinely produce sets of projections of the population of major countries. Projections are also calculated by statistical agencies and academic centers in many countries.

The emergence of such devices as population projection has coincided with more abstract developments in the science of demography. Early in this century, Alfred J. Lotka showed that the arithmetic used in projection had an interesting mathematical implication: if a closed population were subject for a long time to unchanging schedules of fertility and mortality, it would inevitably come to have a constant rate of increase, constant birth and death rates, and a fixed proportionate age distribution, all independent of remote initial conditions. Lotka called this the stable population. (Lotka's formula relating the age distribution to the life table and the rate of increase was the same as the 1760 equation of Euler's used by Malthus in 1824; however, Lotka proved that the continuation of fixed fertility and mortality would produce the fixed–age distribution that Euler had presented). The stable population concepts have proved useful in various forms of demographic estimation, and have been generalized to cover populations with variable as well as with fixed fertility and mortality.

Another part of the developing science has been the calculation of "model" tables of mortality, fertility and marriage. Model tables incorporate the typical age pattern of the relevant demographic variable in schedules that vary in certain parameters, such as the expectation of life at birth, or the mean and variance of the age schedule of fertility or first marriage. The model schedules are calculated from empirical data of apparent high accuracy. They are useful in correcting errors such as omission of events or misstatement of age, and in estimating future schedules of fertility or mortality.

These instances of scientific innovations in demography in the last 50 or 100 years have occurred in demographic research centers located in universities, institutions within governments, and international agencies. In a cursory scan of a mailing list I found demographic centers within governments in nearly 60 countries, in all continents. Among the best known and most productive are the US Bureau of the Census, the UK Registrar-General's Office, and the French Institut National d'Etudes Demographiques, but many other countries have institutions of outstanding quality. Population research is also conducted by international agencies such as the Population Division of the UN, the World Bank, and the World Health Organization. The science has been enhanced at least as much by research in universities around the world, often with the financial support of private foundations. Productive centers in the United States include Brown, Chicago, Columbia, Cornell, Duke, Harvard, Johns Hopkins, Michigan, North Carolina, Pennsylvania, Penn State, Princeton, Stanford, the University of California at Berkeley, and Wisconsin, to list just those that immediately come to mind. In England there are demographic centers in Oxford, Cambridge, the London School of Economics, the London School of Hygiene and Tropical Medicine, and a number of other universities. Basic advances have been produced by the faculty and students at these institutions, and from universities in France, Germany, Italy, and many other countries in Europe, Asia, Australia, Africa, and Latin America.

XVI

CONCLUSION

IN THIS AUTOBIOGRAPHY I have described selected features of my life and of the circumstances in which I have lived and worked. It has been a life blessed with exceptional good fortune, in both my professional and personal experience. My personal good luck includes splendid parents (and a miraculously special aunt), a wife who combines beauty with honesty, intelligence, affection, and very good taste. My professional good fortune involves a career in a fascinating field that was at a wonderful stage when I entered it (as described in the last section), excellent general education from first grade through graduate school, and a wartime career that involved fascinating immersion in electronics. Also I was one of the first persons trained in demography by one of the outstanding pioneers in the field at the first university-based research and training center established in a top ranked postgraduate institution. Other opportunities include teaching brilliant and well–motivated students who have been exceptionally productive. In short, my happy and satisfying life (at least so far) has been possible because of almost unique good luck.

CURRICULUM VITAE

PLACE AND DATE OF BIRTH:
Baltimore, Maryland—November 14, 1917

EDUCATION:
Princeton University—B.A.—1939
Princeton University—M.A.—1941
Princeton University—Ph.D.—1947

ACADEMIC POSITIONS:
Research Assistant at the Office of Population Research, 1941–1942
Instructor, Electrical Communications, Massachusetts Institute of Technology, 1943–1944
Assistant Professor of Economics, Princeton University, 1947–1954
Associate Professor of Economics, Princeton University, 1954–1959
Professor of Economics, Princeton University, 1959–1986
William Church Osborn Professor of Public Affairs, 1964–1986
Assistant Director, Office of Population Research, 1954–1959
Director, Office of Population Research, 1959–1975
Associate Director, Office of Population Research, 1975–1986
Senior Research Demographer, Office of Population Research, 1986–
Visiting Professor, Graduate Program in Demography, University of California, Berkeley, 1987
Visiting Professor, University la Sapienza, Rome, Feb. 1990

OTHER PROFESSIONAL POSITIONS:
United States Navy Reserve, 1941–1946 (Radar Officer)
Secretary, Committee on Social Implications of Atomic Energy, Social Science Research Council, 1946–1947
Member of the Institute for Advanced Study from 1948 to 1950 sponsored by the S.S.R.C. and the National Research Council
U.S. Representative to the U.N. Population Commission, 1961–67.

AWARDS, HONORS:
Fellow, American Academy of Arts and Sciences, American Statistical Association, American Association for the Advancement of Science
Member, American Philosophical Society, American Academy of Arts and Sciences, National Academy of Sciences
Awarded Mindel Sheps Prize in Mathematical Demography, 1974
Doctorat Honoris Causa, University of Louvain, 1979
Honorary Member, Czechoslovak Demographic Society, 1981
Fellow, Center for Advanced Study in the Behavioral Sciences, Stanford, California, September 1982–June 1983
Docteur Honoris Causa, University of Liege, 1983
LLD., University of Pennsylvania, Philadelphia, Pennsylvania, 1983
Corresponding Fellow, British Academy, 1984

Awarded Irene Tauber Prize, 1989
DhL, Princeton University, 1994

PROFESSIONAL ACTIVITIES:
Chairman, S.S.R.C.'s Committee on Social Aspects of Technological Change, 1950–1951.
Consultant, The Rand Corporation, 1951–1953.
Research Mission to India, on population growth and economic development, 1955
   Research Mission to Mexico, on population growth and economic development, 1956
   Rapporteur, U.N. Roundtable on the Uses of Census Data for Social and Economic
   Planning in the ECAFE Region (Bombay), 1960 United States Representative,
   Population Commission of the United Nations, 1961–1968.
Visiting Lecturer, Harvard University, 1962–1965.
Member, Population Committee, National Academy of Sciences, 1963–1966.
Member, Research Advisory Committee, Office of Scientific Personnel, National Research
   Council, 1964.
Consultant to U.N. Special Fund with respect to support of program at CELADE, in
   Santiago (Latin American demographic training center, Santiago), 1964.
Member of Population Council Mission to Kenya, invited by government to evaluate
   demographic situation and recommend policies, 1965.
Member, Technical Advisory Committee for Population, U.S. Bureau of the Census, 1965–
   1969.
Consultant to Population Institute at Haceteppe University (Ankara) on research and
   training program, 1967.
Member of Population Council Mission to Morocco, invited by government to evaluate
   demographic situation and recommend policies, 1967.
Member, Population Council Fellowship Selection Committee, 1968–1970.
Consultant to Ford Foundation on its population program in Latin America (Brazil, Chile),
   1968.
Visit to Indonesia to advise AID on assistance in population to that country, 1969.
Foreign Adviser to Pakistan Institute of Development Economics, 1969.
Member, Advisory Council, National Institute of Child Health and Human Development,
   1969–1973.
Member, International Advisory Committee, East-West Population Institute, 1969–1970.
Invited Expert, U.N. Conference on the measurement of changes in fertility (Budapest,
   1971).
Member, President's Commission on Federal Statistics, 1970–1971.
Member, Population Council Advisory Committee, 1970–1971.
Head of mission to Zaire for U.S. National Academy of Science, for exchange of technical
   information on population, 1971–1972.
Invited Expert, U.N. Ad Hoc Committee on Model Life Tables (New York) 1972.
Chairman, Organizing Committee for Conference on Economic Demography of the
   International Economic Association, 1973.
Senior Adviser, United States Delegation, World Population Conference, Bucharest, 1974.
Chairman, IUSSP Committee on Comparative Analysis of Fertility, 1975–1978.
Consultant, International Institute for Applied Systems Analysis, Vienna, 1976.
Chairman, Committee on Population and Demography, National Academy of Sciences,
   1977–1983.
Member, Program Steering Committee, World Fertility Survey, 1977–1984.
Chairman, Ad Hoc Committee on Illustrative Analyses of World Fertility Survey Results,
   1978–1980.

Member of Panels on Thailand and Egypt, National Academy of Sciences Committee on
 Population and Demography, 1978–1981.
Consultant UNFPA, on establishment of research and training in Demography in the
 People's Republic of China, 1980.
Member, Advisory Committee, International Awards Program on the Determinants of
 Fertility in Developing Countries, Population Council, 1981–1984 (Chairman, 1981–
 1983).

ELECTED OFFICES IN PROFESSIONAL SOCIETIES:
Vice President, President, Population Association of America (1963–1964 and 1967–1968).
Vice President, President, International Union for the Scientific Study of Population (1973–
 1977 and 1977–1981).

PUBLICATIONS:
BOOKS:
The Problem of Reducing Vulnerability to Atomic Bombs. Princeton University Press, 1947,
 116 pp.
Notestein, Taeuber, Kirk, Coale, and Kiser. *The Future Population of Europe and the Soviet
 Union.* Geneva, League of Nations, 1944, 315 pp.
Staff of M.I.T. Radar School, *Principles of Radar.* New York: McGraw-Hill, 1946.
 (Contributor).
T. J. Koopmans, ed. *Activity Analysis of Production and Allocation.* New York: John Wiley,
 1951, pp. 277–279. (Contributor).
Coale, A.J. and Hoover, E.M. *Population Growth and Economic Development in Low-Income
 Countries.* Princeton University Press, 1958, 389 pp.
"Introduction" and "The Effect of Population Change in Aggregate Demand, Prices, and the
 Level of Employment" in *Demographic and Economic Change in Developed Countries.*
 National Bureau of Economic Research, Princeton University Press, 1960, pp. 3–14,
 163–166, 352–371.
Zelnik, M. and Coale, A.J. *New Estimates of Population and Fertility in the United States.*
 Princeton University Press, 1963, 186 pp.
Coale, A.J. and Demeny, P. *Regional Model Life Tables and Stable Populations.* Princeton
 University Press, 1966, 869 pp.
Coale, A.J. and Demeny, P. *Methods of Estimating Basic Demographic Measures from
 Incomplete Data.* United Nations, *Population Studies* No. 42, New York, 1967, 126 pp.
Coale, Brass, Demeny, Heisel, Lorimer, Romaniuk, and van de Walle. *The Demography of
 Tropical Africa.* Princeton University Press, 1968, 539 pp.
The Growth and Structure of Human Population. Princeton University Press, 1972, 227 pp.
Human Fertility in Russia Since the Nineteenth Century (with B. Anderson and E. Härm).
 Princeton University Press, 1979.
Demeny, P. and Coale, A.J. *Regional Model Life Tables and Stable Populations* (Second
 Edition). Academic Press, 1983.
Coale, A.J. and Watkins, S., Co-Editors. *The Decline of Fertility in Europe.* Princeton
 University Press, 1986, 484 pp.

ARTICLES:
"The Problem of Reducing Vulnerability to Atomic Bombs." *American Economic Review,*
 Vol. XXXVII, No. 2 (May 1947): 87–97.
"The Population of the United States in 1950 Classified by Age, Sex, and Color—A Revision
 of the Census Figures." *Journal of the American Statistical Association,* Vol. 50, No. 269
 (March 1955): 16–54.

"The Calculation of Approximate Intrinsic Rates," *Population Index* 21(2):94–97 (April 1955).

"The Effect of Declines in Mortality on Age Distribution," pp. 125–132, Milbank Memorial Fund, *Trends and Differentials in Mortality*, New York, 1956.

"The Effects of Changes in Mortality and Fertility on Age Composition," *Milbank Memorial Fund Quarterly*, XXXIV (1):79–114 (January 1956).

"Age Distribution as Affected by Changes in Fertility and Mortality—A Further Note," *Milbank Memorial Fund Quarterly*, XXXV (3): 302–307, July 1957.

"How the Age Distribution of a Human Population is Determined, "*Proceedings of the Cold Spring Harbor Symposia on Quantitative Biology*, June 1957.

Discussion of Bourgeois-Pichat's paper, "Utilisation de la Notion de Population Stable Pour Mésurer la Mortalité et la Fecondité des Populations des Pays Sous-Développés," *Proceedings of the International Statistical Institute*, Stockholm, August 1957.

"A New Method for Calculating Lotka's—The Intrinsic Rate of Growth in a Stable Population," *Population Studies*, Vol XI, No. 1, July 1957.

"Increases in Expectation of Life and Population Growth," Proceedings of the International Union for the Scientific Study of Population, Vienna, 1959, pp. 36–41.

"Un imperativo per i paesi arretrati: ridure la natalitá," Mercurio 3 (6): 5–11, June 1960.

"Population Density and Growth," *Science* 133 (3468): 1931 ff. June 16, 1961.

"Population Growth," *Science* 134 (3482): 827–829, September 22, 1961.

"The Significance of Age-Patterns of Fertility in High Fertility Populations," (with C. Y. Tye) *Milbank Memorial Fund Quarterly*, 39 (4): 631–646, October 1961.

"The Design of an Experimental Procedure for Obtaining Accurate Vital Statistics," in International Union for the Scientific Study of Population, *International Population Conference Proceedings*, Vol. 2, pp. 372–376, New York, 1961.

"The Case of the Indians and the Teen-Age Widows," (with F. F. Stephan). *Journal of the American Statistical Association*, 57 (298): 338–347, June 1962.

"Estimates of Various Demographic Measures Through the Quasi-Stable Age Distribution," in Milbank Memorial Fund Proceedings of the 39th Annual Conference, *Emerging Techniques in Population Research*, New York, 1963, pp. 175–193.

"World Population Problems" in National Academy of Sciences Committee on Science and Public Policy. Panel on Population Problems. *The Growth of World Population* (Washington, 1963) pp. 8–19.

(Contributor) Roy Greep, ed., *Human Fertility and Population Problems*, Cambridge, Massachusetts, Schenkman Publishing Company, 1963, pp. 143–176. "The Economic Effects of Fertility Control in Underdeveloped Areas."

(Contributor) Philip M. Hauser, ed., *The Population Dilemma*, New York, Prentice Hall for the American Assembly 1963, pp. 46–69. "Population and Economic Development."

(Contributor) C. W. Bray, ed., *Social Science Research and National Security*, "Population Research and the National Interest." Published for Restricted Circulation, 1964.

"How Population Gets Older or Younger." Published by the U.S. State Department in *Forum*, and in a book of essays edited by Ronald Freedman, 1964.

"World Population Problems," in *The Growth of World Population*, National Academy of Sciences Committee on Science and Public Policy, A Panel on Population Problems, Washington, D.C., 1963, pp. 8–19.

"Changes in Statistics on Reproduction," *Population Index*, April 1965, pp. 139–140.

"Population and Economic Development," pp. 27–54, in Universita di Firenze, Scuola di Statistica, *Economia e popolazione: atti del seminario di demografia tenuto nell'anno accademico 1963–64 a cura del Prof. Pierfrancesco Bandettini*, Florence, 1965, 113 pp.

"Factors Associated with the Development of Low Fertility: An Historic Summary." Paper presented at United Nations World Population Conference, Belgrade, Yugoslavia, 1965.

"Estimates of Fertility and Mortality in Tropical Africa," *Population Index*, Vol. 32, No. 2, pp. 173–181.

"Population Trends and Population Control," in Jacinto Steinhardt, ed., *Science and the Modern World*, Plenum Press, 1966, pp. 133–145.

"Convergence of a Human Population to a Stable Form," *Journal of the American Statistical Association*, June 1968.

"Should the United States Start a Campaign for Fewer Births?" *Population Index*, Vol. 34, No. 3, October-December 1968 (Presidential address at the annual meeting of the Population Association of America, 1968), pp. 467–474.

"Conclusion," summary of conference on Population Growth and Economic Development in Africa held in Nairobi in December 1969, ibid., pp. 397–400.

"The Decline of Fertility in Europe from the French Revolution to World War II," *Fertility and Family Planning: A World View*, S. J. Behrman, M.D., Leslie Corsa, Jr., M.D., Ronald Freedman (eds.), The University of Michigan, A Sesquicentennial Publication, The University of Michigan Press, Ann Arbor, 1969, pp. 388–412.

"World Population: Large and Getting Larger," *The Christian Family in Today's World*, The Foundation for International Cooperation, Chicago, Illinois, 1969, pp. 16–19.

"Findings of the Conference and Suggestions for Further Research," *Turkish Demography: Proceedings of a Conference*, Frederic C. Shorter and Bozkurt Guvenc (eds.), Hacettepe University Publications No. 7, Hacettepe University Institute of Population Studies, Ankara, Turkey, 1969, pp. 299–307.

"The Use of Fourier Analysis to Express the Relation Between Time Variations in Fertility and the Time Sequence of Births in a Closed Human Population," *Demography*, Vol. 7, No. 1, February 1970, pp. 93–120.

"Man and His Environment," *Science*, Vol. 170, pp. 132–136, Oct. 9, 1970.

Book Review of *Population, Resources, Environment, Issues in Human Ecology*, by Paul R. Ehrlich and Anne H. Ehrlich, in *Science*, October 23, 1970, Vol. 170, No. 3956, pp. 428–429.

"Rates and Proportions Resulting from the Combination of Age-Specific Experience or Characteristics with Different Stable Age Distributions," *The Proceedings of the International Union for the Scientific Study of Population*, Liege, 1971.

"Age Patterns of Marriage," *Population Studies*, Vol. 25 (July 1971) pp. 193–214.

"The Determination of Vital Rates in the Absence of Registration Data," *Milbank Memorial Fund Quarterly* (Forty Years of Research in Human Fertility, edited by C. V. Kiser), Vol. 49, Part 2 (October 1971) pp. 230–234.

"Constructing the Age Distribution of a Population Recently Subject to Declining Mortality," *Population Index*, Vol. 37 (April–June 1971) pp. 75–82.

"Determination of Vital Rates in the Absence of Registration Data," *Milbank Quarterly*, October 1971, Vol. XLIX, No. 4, Part 2, pp. 175–187.

"The Demography of Constantly Changing Birth Rates," in *Spatial, Regional and Population Economics*, edited by Mark Perlman, Charles Leven & Benjamin Chinitz, 1972, New York: Gordon & Breach.

(with H. J. Page) "Fertility & Child Mortality South of the Sahara," in *Population Growth & Economic Development in Africa*, edited by S. H. Ominde and C. N. Ejiogu. Published by Heinemann, London/Nairobi/ Ibadan in association with the Population Council, New York, 1972, pp. 51–66.

(with D. R. McNeil) "The Distribution by Age of First Marriage in a Female Cohort," *Journal of the American Statistical Association*, December 1972, Vol. 67, No. 340, pp. 743–749.

"Alternative Paths to a Stationary Population," *Demographic and Social Aspects of Population Growth*, Charles F. Westoff and Robert Parke, Jr., eds., Research Reports of the Commission on Population Growth and the American Future, Vol. 1, Washington, D.C.: Government Printing Office, pp. 589–603.

"A Statistical Reconstruction of the Black Population of the United States 1880–1970: Estimate of True Numbers by Age and Sex, Birth Rates, and Total Fertility," *Population Index* 39(1):3–36, January 1973 (with Norfleet W. Rives, Jr.).

"The Demographic Transition Reconsidered," *Proceedings* of the International Union for the Scientific Study of Population, Liege 1973.

"Age Composition in the Absence of Mortality and in Other Odd Circumstances," *Demography*, Vol. 10, No. 4, November 1973.

"Model Fertility Schedules: Variations in the Age Structure of Childbearing in Human Populations," *Population Index* 40(2):185–258, April 1974 (with T. James Trussell).

"Interview/Ansley J. Coale: Too many People?" *Challenge*, Sept–Oct, 1974.

"The History of the Human Population," *Scientific American* 231(3):40, September 1974.

"A New Method of Estimating Standard Fertility Measures from Incomplete Data," *Population Index* 41(2):182–210, April 1975 (with T. James Trussell and Allan Hill).

"Methods of Estimating Births, Deaths, and Marriages in Less Well Developed Countries," *Proceedings* of 40th Session of the International Statistical Institute, Warsaw, September 1–9, 1975.

"On the Asymptotic Trajectory of the Roots of Lotka's Equation," *Theoretical Population Biology*, Vol. 9, No. 1, February 1976 (with D. R. McNeil).

"Introduction," Economic Factors in Population Growth, edited by Ansley J. Coale, pp. xi–xviii, London: The Macmillan Press Ltd., 1976.

"A Reassessment of the Demography of Traditional Rural China," (with George W. Barclay, Michael A. Stoto, and T. James Trussell) *Population Index*, 42 (October 1976): 606–635.

"The Development of New Models of Nuptiality and Fertility," *Population*, numero special (September 1977):131–150.

"Population Growth and Economic Development: The Case of Mexico." *Foreign Affairs* 56: 415–429, 1978.

"T. R. Malthus and the Population Trends in His Day and Ours," *Encyclopedia Britannica Lecture 1978*, The University of Edinburgh.

"The Quality of Data in the Nepal Fertility Survey," (with Noreen Goldman and Maxine Weinstein) *Scientific Reports* #6, 38 pp. December 1979.

"Reflections on the Helsinki Conference on Economic and Demographic Change." (with Aarno Strommer and Aimo Pulkkinen) *Yearbook of Population Research in Finland* 1979. The Population Research Institute, Helsinki.

"The Use of Modern Analytical Demography by T. R. Malthus." *Population Studies* Vol. 33, No. 2, October 1979.

Biographical Sketch of Frank W. Notestein, for supplement to *International Encyclopedia of the Social Sciences*, published in 1979.

Preface to the proceedings of the International Union for the Scientific Study of Population, Seminar on Natural Fertility, edited by Henri Leridon and Jane Menken, Liege, 1979.

"A General Model for Analyzing the Effect of Nuptiality on Fertility," (with T. James Trussell and Jane Menken). Published in *Nuptiality and Fertility*, Proceedings of an IUSSP Seminar held in Bruges, Belgium, January 1979. L.T. Ruzicka, Editor. Ordina Editions, 1982. pp. 7–27.

"Nuptiality and Fertility in the Republic of Korea," (with Noreen Goldman and Lee-Jay Cho). Published in *Nuptiality and Fertility*, Proceedings of an IUSSP Seminar held in Bruges, Belgium, January 1979. L.T. Ruzicka, Editor. Ordina Editions, 1982. pp. 43–60.

"The Estimation of Recent Trends in Fertility and Mortality in the Republic of Korea," (with Lee-Jay Cho and Noreen Goldman). Committee on Population and Demography, National Research Council, published by the National Academy of Sciences, Washington, D.C., 77 pp., 1980.

"Critical Scrutiny of RPFS First Country Report Data," in *Proceedings* of the National Seminar on the 1978 Republic of the Philippines Fertility 81 Survey, Manila, December 17–18, 1979, pp. 26–34 (August 1980).

"Estimating the Completeness of Reporting Adult Deaths in Populations that are Approximately Stable," *Population Index*, 46(2):179–202. 1980.

"Introduction, Remarriage and the Matrimonial Market. A Methodological Approach." (Edited by J. Dupaquier et. al). London: Academic Press 1981.

"Robust Estimation of Fertility by the Use of Model Stable Populations." Published in *Asian and Pacific Census Forum*, Vol. 8, No. 2, East-West Population Institute, November 1981 Also published in CELADE journal "Notas de Poblacion," No. 26, August 1981.

"Population Trends, Population Policy, and Population Studies in China," *Population and Development Review*, Vol. 7, No. 1, pp. 85–97, March 1981.

"A Further Note on Chinese Population Statistics," *Population and Development Review*, Vol. 7, No. 3, pp. 512–518, September 1981.

"Roots, or How a Population Forgets Its Past," (with James Trussell). *Canadian Studies in Population* 8(1981):1–25. 1981.

"A Reassessment of World Population Trends", *Population Bulletin of the U.N.* 14:1–16, 1982. Paper presented at the IUSSP General Conference, Manila, December 1981.

"Duration-Specific Marital Fertility in Egypt," (with Shafik El-Atoum), Population Bulletin of ECWA, No. 22/23, June and December 1982.

"Age Structure, Growth, Attrition, and Accession: A New Synthesis," (with S. H. Preston). *Population Index* 48, No. 2, Summer 1982.

"A Simple Equation for Estimating the Expectation of Life at Old Ages," *Population Studies* 36(2):317–326. 1982.

"The Estimation of Recent Trends in Fertility and Mortality in Egypt," Report of the Panel on Egypt, Committee on Population and Demography. Published by the National Academy Press, 1982. Report #9.

"Age Patterns of Mortality for Older Persons," (with Shiro Horiuchi). Paper presented at 1983 Meetings of the Population Association of America.

"Recent Trends in Fertility in Less Developed Countries," *Science*, 221: 828–832. 1983.

"Population Trends in China and India" (A Review), *Proceedings* of the National Academy of Sciences, Vol. 80, pp. 1757–1763, March 1983.

"A Biography of Frank W. Notestein," *Population Index* 49, No. 1, Spring 1983.

"Rapid Population Change in China, 1952–1982." Report No. 27 of the Committee on Population and Demography, National Research Council. National Academy Press, 1984.

"Life Table Construction on the Basis of Two Enumerations of a Closed Population. *Population Index*, 50(2):193–213. 1984.

"The Demographic Transition." *Pakistan Development Review.* 23(4):531–52. 1984.

"Biographical Memoir of Frank W. Notestein." In *American Philosophical Society Yearbooks-1984.*

"Fertility in Pre-revolutionary China: In Defense of a Reassessment." *Population and Development Review.* 10(3):471–480. 1984.

"Two Sets of County Boundaries, and Erroneous Figures for County Vital Rates in Nineteenth-Century Ireland." (with Edith Pantelides). Published in Teitelbaum, Michael S. *The British Fertility Decline: Demographic Transition in the Crucible of the Industrial Revolution.* Princeton: Princeton University Press, pp. 228–245. 1984.

"An Extension and Simplification of a New Synthesis of Age Structure and Growth." *Asian and Pacific Census Forum*, 12(1):5–8. Aug, 1985.

"Fertility in Rural China: A Reconfirmation of the Barclay Reassessment." In Susan B. Hanley and Arthur P. Wolf (eds.). *Family and Population in East Asian History.* Stanford, California, Stanford University Press, pp. 185–95. 1985.

"A Reply to Kim's Comment." *Population Index.* Spring:51(1):6–9. 1985.

"Estimation of Expectation of Life at Advanced Ages." *Genus.* 40(3–4):185–190. 1985.

"Calculation of Age-Specific Fertility Schedules from Tabulations of Parity in Two Censuses." (with A. Meredith John and Toni Richards). *Demography* 22(7): 611–623. 1985.

"Nuclear War and Demographers' Projections." *Population and Development Review.* 11(3): 483–493. 1985.

"Demographic Effects of Scientific Progress." Papers read at the Joint Meeting of the Royal Society and the American Philosophical Society, April 1986. Volume I.

"Mortality Crossovers: Reality or Bad Data?" (with Ellen E. Kisker). *Population Studies* 40(3): 389–401. 1986.

"Population Trends and Economic Development." (in Jane Menken, ed.). *World Population and U.S. Policy: The Choices Ahead.* Chap. 3, pp. 110–126. New York: W. W. Norton. 1986.

"A Summary of the Changing Distribution of Overall Fertility, Marital Fertility, and the Proportion Married in the Provinces of Europe." (with R. Treadway). In *The Decline of Fertility in Europe.* Princeton University Press, 1986:31–181.

"The Decline of Fertility in Europe Since the Eighteenth Century as a Chapter in Demographic History." Princeton University Press, 1986:31–181.

"Demographic Effects of Below-Replacement Fertility and Their Social Implications." *Population and Development Review.* 1986: (Suppl):203–216.

"Age Intervals and Time Intervals: Reply to Kim." (with S. Preston) *Demography*, 23(3):463–465.

"Basic Data on Fertility in the Provinces of Mainland China, 1940–1982." (with Chen, Sheng Li). *Papers of the East-West Population Institute*, No. 104, Jan. 1987.

Review of *Population Growth and Economic Development: Policy Questions* by the National Research Council, Committee on Population, Working Group on Population Growth and Economic Development. *Journal of Political Economy*, 95(4):887–892. August 1987.

"As Implicaçes Sociais de Fecundidade Abaixo do Nível de Substituiço." *Revista Brasileira de Estudos de Populaço*, 4(1):39–60. 1987

"Defects in Data on Old Age Mortality in the United States: New Procedures for Calculating Approximately Accurate Mortality Schedules and Life Tables at the Highest Ages." (with Ellen E. Kisker). Study conducted for the National Center of Health Statistics. *Asian and Pacific Population Forum*, 4(1). Spring, 1990.

"Fertility Change in the People's Republic of China and Selected Other East Asian Populations: Similarities and Differences." (with Ron Freedman). Presented at the IUSSP seminar in Bangkok, Spring 1988. *Asian and Pacific Census Forum.*

"The Distribution of Interbirth Intervals in Rural China, 1940's–1970's." (with Shaomin Li and Jing-Qing Han). *Papers of the East-West Population Institute*, No. 109, August 1988.

"Fertility and Mortality in Different Populations with Special Attention to China." *Proceedings of the American Philosophical Society*, 132(2):185–195. 1988.

"A Reassessment of Fertility Trends, Taking Account of the Egyptian Fertility Survey." Chapter 1 in *Egypt: Demographic Responses to Modernization*, A. Hallouda, S. Farid, S. Cochrane, eds. Central Agency for Public Mobilisation and Statistics, Cairo, 1988.

"Marriage and Childbearing in China Since 1940." *Social Forces*, 67(4):833–850. June 1989.

"Revised Regional Model Life Tables at Very Low Levels of Mortality." *Population Index* 55(4):613–643. 1989. (with Guang Guo).

"The Demographic Transition and its Implications for Population Trends in the Less Developed Countries," and "Population Growth and Economic Development: Coale and Hoover Re-examined after 25 Years," *Lectures in Development Economics*, No. 8, 1990. Pakistan Institute of Development Economics.

"Age Patterns of Mortality for Older Women: An Analysis Using the Age-specific Rate of Mortality Change with Age." *Mathematical Population Studies*, 2(4):245–267. 1990. Shiro Horiuchi and A.J. Coale.

"Recent Trends in Fertility and Nuptiality in China." *Science*, Jan. 1991. (with Wang Feng, Nancy E. Riley and Lin Fu De).

"The Use of New Model Life Tables at Very Low Mortality in Population Projection," *Population Bulletin of the United Nations*, No. 31, 1991. (with Guang Guo).

"The Effect of Age Misreporting in China on the Calculation of Mortality Rates at Very High Ages." *Demography*, 28(2):293–301. (with Shaomin Li). May 1991.

"Estimation of the Number of Persons at Advanced Ages from the Number of Deaths at Each Age in the Given Year and Adjacent Years." *Genus*, 56(1–2):1–24, 1990. (with Graziella Caselli).

"Excess Female Mortality and the Balance of the Sexes in the Population: An Estimate of the Number of "Missing Females." *Population and Development Review*, 17(3):517–523. Sept. 1991.

"Some Relations among Cultural Traditions, Nuptiality and Fertility. *The Pakistan Development Review*, 30(4):397–406. Winter 1991.

"An Analysis of the Nepal Fertility Survey Maternity Histories," pp. 315–346 in Allan G. Hill and William Brass (eds.) *The Analysis of Maternity Histories*. International Union for the Scientific Study of Population, Liège, Belgium: Ordina Editions, 1992. (with Noreen Goldman and Maxine Weinstein).

"Age of Entry into Marriage and the Date of the Initiation of Voluntary Birth Control." *Demography*, 29(3):333–341. August, 1992.

"The Possible Future of Mortality in Europe and North America," paper prepared for 1992 conference in Amsterdam on Prospects in Next Century for Former U.S.S.R.

"Future Population Trends and Policy Responses," paper prepared for Expert Group Meeting on Population Policies and Programmes, Cairo, Egypt 12–16. April 1992.

Similarities in the Fertility Transition in China and Three Other East Asian Populations. Chapter 12 in *The Revolution in Asian Fertility*. Edited by Richard Leete and Iqbal Alam. Clarendon Press: Oxford. 1992. (With Ronald Freedman)

"Nuptiality and Fertility in USSR Republics and Neighboring Populations," pp. 3–17 in Wolfgang Lutz, Sergei Scherbov and Andrei Volkov (eds.) *Demographic Trends and Patterns in the Soviet Union Before 1991*. International Institute for Applied Systems Analysis, Laxenburg, Austria: 1994.

"Five Decades of Missing Females in China." *Demography* 31(3). August 1994.

"The Present Status of the World Population, of Demography, and Population Policy," Forward, in Oscar Harkavy, *Curbing Population Growth*. Plenum: New York, 1995.

"Age Patterns and Time Sequence of Mortality in National Populations with the Highest Expectation of Life at Birth," *Population and Development Review*, forthcoming.

Ansley J. Coale

*Summer 1950, with our sons
Ansley Jr., and Rob*

*The Grand Hotel Golden Dragon Room
December 17, 1981*

My Grandfather, James J. Coale,
Pastor at the Toms River
Presbyterian Church around 1900

My mother, Nellie Ansley Johnson,
in Fairland around 1900

My father, James J. Coale, Jr., holding my brother Jim and me, 1919

Father holding me

My sister Virginia, brother Jim, and me, Govens, Maryland, 1918

Jim and me at Severna Park about 1926

*Jim, me, and dog (Lassie)
at Hockley, three miles
from Annapolis, 1928*

*Napolean on front steps of house on
Franklin Street, Annapolis*

Ansley as an undergraduate at Princeton, 1939

Jim and I shooting marbles in backyard in Cleveland, 1927

*Sue with Pete and me at
12 Sumner Road, Cambridge, 1943*

*Sue, Ansley, and Sue's sister Holly,
Summer 1943*

Sue and Ansley holding Pete, Cambridge 1943

*My friend of the
Taney Avenue Gang,
Pete Fox, and his wife,
Sue's sister*

Pete and me 1943

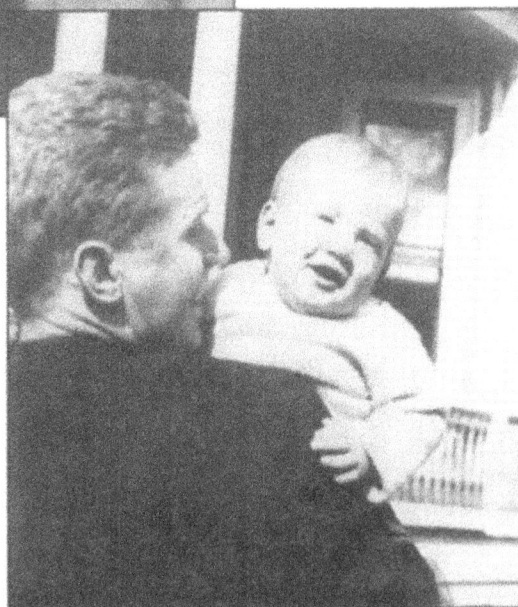

With the President of Sri Lanka, and Sir Maurice Kendall, 1978,
(in connection with discussion of the results of the world fertility survey in Sri Lanka)

Receiving honorary degree,
at Louvain La Neuve, 1979

At the Population Commission of the United Nations, with Howard Brumman,
advisor from the Bureau of the Census, and John Borham, 1964

Meeting with Vice Premier Chen Muhua in the Hall of the People
in Beijing, on mission to China in 1980

*Farewell on his retirement by
graduate students*

In the fitness center

*Reading to his older granddaughter,
Sarah*

Sue and our granddaughters,
Sarah and Dena

Meeting of the Council of the International Union for the
scientific study of population, Manila, 1979, Mercedes Cenception in the chair

Graziella, Italy, 1990

Party in Florence at IUSSP Meeting, 1985

*Receiving honorary degree, at
University of Pennsylvania, 1983*

*Walter Daub and Ansley at 50th Reunion
of the Class of 1939, 1989*

Receiving honorary degree at Princeton, 1994

INDEX